Point
and Line

THALIA FIELD

Point and Line

A NEW DIRECTIONS BOOK

Pieces from this book have appeared in earlier forms in the following places: Excerpt from "Hours," *Language aLive* (#5), Guest-editor: Caroline Bergvall, Published by Sound&Language (Lowestoft, 1999, England). "Seven Veils," *Conjunctions*:33, edited by Bradford Morrow, fall 1999. "Hours," *NuMuse*, edited by Aishah Rahman, 1998. "Coming-of-Age," *Central Park* #26, edited by Stephen-Paul Martin, 1997. "Walking Home," *Conjunctions*:26, edited by Bradford Morrow, 1996. "A∴I," FC2's *On the Edge: New Women's Fiction Anthology*, edited by Chris Mazza, 1995. "The Compass Room," *Avec*, edited by Cydney Chadwick, 1995.

Manufactured in the United States of America
Book design by Sylvia Frezzolini Severance
New Directions Books are printed on acid-free paper.
First published as New Directions Paperbook 899 in 2000
Published simultaneously in Canada by Penguin Books Canada

Library of Congress Cataloging-in-Publication Data

Field, Thalia, 1966–
    Point and line/Thalia Field
      p. cm.
    ISBN 0-8112-1442-7
    I. Title.

PS3556.I398 P6 2000
811'.54—dc21   99-089048

New Directions Books are published for James Laughlin
by New Directions Publishing Corporation
80 Eighth Avenue, New York 10011

for Natalie, Harriet, and Marion

■

There exists still another force which develops not within the point, but outside it. This force hurls itself upon the point which is digging its way into the surface, tears it out and pushes it about the surface in one direction or another. The concentric tension of the point is thereby immediately destroyed and, as a result, it perishes and a new being arises out of it which leads a new, independent life in accordance with its own laws. This is the Line.

■ Wassily Kandinsky

CONTENTS

OUTLINE, IN MIND

A ∴ I

I occupy this comfortable chair in your office and you stare at me. We are not speaking to one another, so you've called this uncomfortable time *silence*.

A cat wanders around your legs.

I rushed here and made it on time to the door, stood outside and turned up late. Now I find it funny you should have produced this thoughtless word. A cat falls from a bookshelf and lands on its feet.

A cat collects itself to jump. A pleasure to watch. A relief to see a creature inhabiting itself comfortably.

I have heard that staring is a predator's first weapon.

A big bang, one first cell, a tiny clue, a kernel of truth, an unrevealed fact that puts all of me in perspective. Your job is to espy and co-author that spot. From beyond the horizon a searchlight seems sourceless and impossible to deflect.

I will keep pointing out the cat. That specific cat, I don't know its name. How easily it slips from the room.

A foghorn intrudes and the lighthouse beam cuts through a marsh. The probing light keeps night ships wary of land — aware of land as an obstacle or a destination.

I am not speaking to you but if you could get beyond that, there is much to celebrate. Minutes have passed. Invisible kicks to the pendulum compensate for the effects of air resistance.

An eye grows accustomed so that vision takes shape in a dark room, though it's been said that the shapes emerge. A basket of plastic flowers looks perfect on your desk.

I count on the fact that in another thirty minutes this episode will end and I'll walk back onto a street where nobody is speaking to me, and yet I would never call it silent.

A girl strolls through a bustling market, walking alone from fence to fence, around the backs of benches, wandering without stalling.

I see another basket, empty of plastic flowers.

A job, what a job — to connect so many carelessly scattered spots. The spread of seeds, the search for new stars. The whole entanglement of sowing and harvest is utterly for the birds — which is why birds are such menaces to the farmers. And big scarecrows guard the broken earth. And swarms of bats suck the night clear of insects.

I mean, the bats hear exactly where we are.

A girl, in your book, is never alone. So I must be the third person here. The girl in an open-air market speaks to no one, as she was taught to do by a protective parent, or by experience. And so she is silent, and so you'd say she and I are identical. Eden is a small town on most maps and yet people pretend not to know it, only allude to it as the first place, the justifiable cause of where we are today.

I won't pick up the looks you flick onto the rug between us. This may be "the most silent you've ever seen me," but your seeing has become suspect since you've made a career out of it. *How many times do you see her? Oh, I see her twice a week.*

A moth saw a flame and thought what it saw was its heart and it said, "What is my heart doing over there, away from me?" And believing that it could not be whole without an organ it had never even used, the moth dove toward it, hoping to reabsorb it in open surgery, but instead there was a sound as empty as a lit match extinguished on water, and in an instant the heart that had stood away from the moth became the central unimagined ecstasy the moth couldn't live without.

I fear that there is no such thing as being naked.

A hood has practical use. A veil. The eyelid is a very sensual place to be kissed. A kiss here, no matter how delicate, shocks the eyeball underneath which doesn't yet think of itself as a physical sphere able to be touched. And the brain doesn't know how this touch feels, there is no word for it. A hood hides a spot in every culture. In some, the concealing is worshipped, in some undone — and you can't tell which — yet you want desperately to find it.

I may squirm with a pleasure I didn't know I had, that you can show me, that is really your pleasure.

A hand skims back and forth causing small ripples in an ocean of bath water.

I won't emerge. The Polaroid wasn't loaded so all that develops is the feeling of panic as we discover that the candids are lost: *"We would have lived life differently had we known the dumb thing was empty!"* A girl is approached by a stranger at the market. He will ask her if she's lost, not where she's going.

A cat pushes his way into the room. He rubs against the couch, and then my knees and then yours, joining us with his attention.

I try and forget how tightly sealed the window is as I focus on the street scene through it, as I focus on squeezing the air from the bottom of my lungs.

A girl searches an open-air market for something to buy with the change in her pocket. Her slow consideration of everything takes on the rhythm of water spilling across a table, growing as vastly clear as sunlight on a blank wall.

I'm going to ask the question at the end of our time, as your hand reaches for the door, "Is that cat alive or dead?"

A hat flies up and a girl loses it in the blinding hole, the sun. It spills on the concrete and she steps off the sidewalk to pick the hat up, looking to see if anyone saw her. An amateur astronomer kneels at the base of his telescope as the glow from a fifteen-million-year-old supernova slowly appears to him.

I feel my cheeks burn as if they might peel off and fly toward the window, striking against it, a terrifying wet bird.

A girl sniffs the gyros from a full block away, remembering the salty oil and the soft wings of meat, desiring them as she approaches the colorful banners. A girl picks her way through the stalls, searching for ways to spend her money. She thought she would buy a scarf, but she has become hungry.

I guess you could say I've brought this situation on myself; sitting here is no different than paying for a parking space when I don't own a car. We don't spend money on words when we put them to waste, so why spend it on the choice not to use them?

A network TV movie languishing unmade, you might say.

I could sell the rights if I could simply tell the story. The relief on your face whenever I toss up a detail! The tastiest ones I have robbed from half-strangers, their open mouths like velvet sacks to pull back before you, leaving a pile of glittering rock sugar, jewels, what you believe is the rarest vein of my soul visible across a table. They sparkle in your eyes and you tackle them efficiently and with style. Suddenly crime seems to pay. Confession is the climax of the seduction. So you lean back and uncross your legs, looking as relaxed as you'd like me to.

"A" sounds like "I" when spoken.

I sort of wish you'd tap that pencil. But that sort of gesture, at some point in your training, has been labeled unprofessional.

A third ring.

I stare at you. The phone rings a fourth time and the answering machine sucks the sound into its plastic body where on turning tape a voice discharges.

A voice is calling you —

I know you want to press the button, lean in, soak up the wet sweet words. However, owing to your professionalism, you can only shoot glances at the clock.

A strategy has prevailed as in all battles; the power of mundanity.

"So how was your weekend?

I know what you mean. I know the story you want — there's that pleasure in driving too fast that in speaking would slow way down and vanish, the motion rolling to a stop with the force of friction if I would try to describe what happened.

A spot like that can't be looked into. A place on the map, a motel for fossils that slip out at night and skulk along the cooled sidewalks, leaning back flat against painted wood, familiar patterns of bones casting Sanskrit shadows.

I know that between any two people in conversation resides the potential to give birth to the world. But could it begin with two like us, sitting in comfortable chairs, not speaking? Who would the epic infant look like, me or you? The fantasy of stealing my mother's baby enters my mind. If this is transference, may I ask you to remove your clothing?

A payment of money for this is ridiculous.

"I surveyed the ceiling of my prison . . . It was the painted figure of Time as he is commonly represented, save that, in lieu of a scythe, he held what, at a casual glance, I supposed to be the picture of a pendulum." You twist the watch around your wrist as though time might gain momentum—

you try again to throw me something: a swath of speech so solid we can both see it, but which, falling, covers more.

"You took care of yourself I hope."

A cat like yours is a Schrödinger's cat, sealed up in an office where someone's disintegration provides a 50-50 chance of its death. *Take care of her*, says the mobster to the hit man, winking verbally. At the end of an hour the lid will be lifted to see the results.

I've never seen you this way. Darkness and a hushed room are alike when you walk into them. A night sky and a silent god have a lot in common.

An irresponsible look brews in your eyes.

I may repeat stories about *a girl* in so many different forms you think you're encountering a life. Maybe you think it's *my* life? Always assume that nothing relates. A girl, the invention of plastic, amateur cosmologists, "I," "you," pieces of paper, my chair, it's just a combination that continues until a stopping place is reached and the time is up, frame busted, and then it continues despite us. The cat sits alive, dead, or whatever it is, just inside the door pulling its claws.

A girl once went to confession and said, *I have never spoken truthfully about myself* to a priest whose eyes widened as he nodded in that fascinating way.

I know you need me to start speaking up before I become dangerous.

A parade of lives roams the street, sealed out. Silent, and yet you don't seem concerned about them.

I lean forward and think we shouldn't see each other any more. I might say I spent the weekend idling outside a motel in an upstate town. Then you would ask me why I came back, and I would think why I was idling. I found an open place and I watched it come into view. A raw motel. A car parked suddenly. A place of clothing. An entrance. If I named my sins they would become obligations. On my back finally opened sideways on a brown bedspread I thought pleasantly of nothing while I gave pleasure with my tongue.

A billboard comes down piece by piece. You thought you heard me say something? A wall, a line, a galaxy, or the flesh of our heads stands between us. Where you see a barrier, there is a place of opportunity.

I do flatter you with a look now and then, which you grab up eagerly like undeserved flowers. In one flower you could hear a thousand words, but you can't read minds, you've often said, trying to keep my gaze from falling back to the window, which of course I let it do.

A room in which walls, ceiling, and floor are totally bare behaves to sound in the same way it would to light if it were lined with mirrors. When two people communicate, their brains begin to mirror each other and the boundaries between them dissolve.

I wonder what it is about darkness that makes us sure we can't move safely through it. Something about bumping into things with our bodies first. That the touch might be painful, erotic, before we understand it.

A pair of cats rushes in — entangled —— a live cat and a dead cat screeching and hissing, baring excruciating flashes of claw. This display brings you to your feet and you chase them away.

"I cautiously moved forward, with my arms extended, and my eyes straining from their sockets, in the hope of catching some faint ray of light." As I get older I lie in fewer words.

A bat, trapped in a house where people are screaming and swatting at it, swoops and narrowly misses them and every silver portrait on the mantle. Around the room it banks and plummets until as it hears the plate-glass window and turns to avoid it, the bat realizes what it hears is always where it heads and wonders, "What is my future doing over there, away from me?" Terrified it won't live to see a future free from the blaring echo of its mind always already in front of it, the bat dives toward the glass, silencing it with constant attention.

I drove through fog on my way north and the headlights made even the tiniest particles of air blaze. I could see best when I turned the lights off completely.

A girl laughed out loud leaving the confession booth where behind the wooden panel the priest had grown angrier, shaking the whole box with outrage as minutes passed and the girl would neither speak nor leave. *Make her do one or the other*, he prayed to God.

I think *window* several times. In the mind, words are heard bone-dry without the benefit of breath.

A billboard rises across the dusty sunset, saying something about buying or driving a new car. In the image I step into a mini-mart for cigarettes and on the way out I spot another billboard where I'm enjoying a good smoke. At night up north I practiced echo-locating off unfamiliar ears.

At first your questions — like flashlights toward Orion — vanished into the paradox of the dark night sky: an infinite universe filled infinitely with stars should make any line of sight eventually hit a star in the sky, strike a word, a memory. This being so, and there being infinite lines of sight, why is the night sky dark and not a screen of burning light?

Edgar Allan Poe thought about this and concluded that time was on his side. The farther into space he looked the further back in time he saw — back to where stories first formed in fiery spit and crashing density — and he realized that even if he couldn't travel the past, he could simply wait and it would come to him. "The only mode, therefore...in which we could comprehend the voids which our telescopes find in innumerable directions, would be by supposing the distance of the invisible background so immense that no ray from it has yet been able to reach us at all."

And the thing I'm counting on is that time is on my side too; that I can sit here for long enough for you to run that clock down and admit a certain defeat with the envelope I'll hand you with your fee. In many ways, we are as gothic as the thick illogical spaces between stars, between good ideas, between motel rooms. For different reasons we may both be right: I am making myself crazy.

A car pulls up outside your building and begins honking.

I traveled alone in a real metal vehicle, the touch of the vinyl, the invitation of familiar music to a foot, a certain weight collecting, bearing down on a pedal connected to a machine I can neither understand nor fix. And yet I accelerated too. The sky was brewing a dark drink as I idled outside the motor lodge.

A girl lost her change and so tries to retrace where she's been, kneeling in the dirt between tables and legs. The temporary booths sway in the heavy breeze, bent nails slide from the soft wood as the tarping whips off. A girl studies faces for the one who has taken her money. So much for the open-air, for the kindness of improvised spaces.

I know you are only a fading echo of Poe and that I, unable to form a counter theory to his, stubbornly occupy a losing position. For you too have faith that at the horizon of what you can see lies *the creation*, awaiting revelation, eventually emerging for your inspection. The farther the light travels, the harder the words come, the more they reflect the original state of things. Numerous but feeble rays whispering the inchoate talking cure of the big bang. Admit it, in my silence you think you see the possibility of everything there is to know about me. A dictionary left on this leather chair when I go would serve you equally in conjuring me up. I refer to this when I say,

"I'm thinking of stopping ..."

A better Poe might have spoken about the universe that moves away from itself at all times, that perhaps has no center, that at all points surges in every direction so the future and the past are only as strong as fences of human hair, catching sparks in the ether.

"I counted the rushing vibrations of the steel! Inch by inch, line by line..."

A false distinction lies between music and the noise of garbage cans pulled along pavement.

I know in the city the sky at night isn't dark at all, and that's one reason this dialogue may never have been possible. When the lights were out and I lay across the brown bedspread, the face that leaned down and touched mine was as empty as a window.

"How long have you felt this way?"

A whole nest of possibilities falls between us and yet you try to save only the already dead. I understand why you look at me the way you do: a boarded up window with a window painted on it; understanding someone is the most irrational contract there is.

I prefer the cat which is now a messy melange of live and dead cats.

A girl runs through the market with the scarf she stole as the booths collapsed. When she reaches an alley where nobody can see her she runs her hands out to the full length of the fabric, folding it around her head.

I feel a constriction in my chest. What can I say to get you to open the window? That kind of transparency is suffocating.

A girl travels in the city unrecognized. Her youth and her face now covered in soft blue printed cotton. She was irrepressible when I first saw her, she is even lighter now.

I am really the criminal you won't say I am. In instance after instance, I kill you. And each procession I hear of myself is a funeral. The hill is muddy, silence surrounds your coffin, and because you are dead, even the patter of the dirt as it touches you is like affection you can't feel. Too bad you have to die in here. Some of me is very sorry and wants to disrupt the killing spree. Some of me wants to torture you because you make it so easy. Some of me is the guard on duty who looks blithely the other way and later denies the whole affair. I am all the murderers who served their silence up cold; can you tell I'm looking at you now —

A vacuum of agreement is between us.

I reach across the two feet of space and lift the window without asking. There is no reverberation as I let the impatient rustle of traffic into this "silent" room.

A sound made in the open air travels away, and for the most part doesn't return.

I hear the street like a reprieve. I am so aware of all the noise outside I can barely look at you. And how is it that you don't know my mind is as loud as your staring at my hands — now that they are refusing to fidget as they have in the past. In the stillness of my hands you suddenly think you hear something.

A star once discovered is given a name. New words come into the language as technology changes, as people change. Still, there are light waves you do not see which go into your mind undetected. There are sounds that flow up through your feet from where I've pushed the earth and it's pushed you back.

I pay you money so that we may share this kind of history.

A car runs smoothly when the teeth of one gear enter and leave the spaces of another.

I read that on the witness stand, the murderer's father appeared guiltier than his son when asked about their Sunday dinners or why he suspected nothing.

A girl looks up through the buildings sensing someone staring. Into the fisheye of a giant telescope on a planet as distant as a pleasant sound, she thumbs her nose and shakes a motor from her tongue. *I know exactly where I am*, she is prepared to say to any gloved hand that stops her.

I can't think of a more sublime torture than a subpoena.

A girl races now, away from her shadow. She dashed past me on the way in here, and I stood for several minutes outside your door, hoping to eventually emerge as her, or at least running that quickly.

I know an instant before it happens that this time is suddenly over.

"Oh!"

A startled noise as the hour jumps to your eyes like a cat to your lap and you turn almost sheepish, raise yourself from the chair. Nervously you indicate the clock, your watch, the door, even the answering machine as though you fear I might linger eternally. You want me to see that everything in the room has conspired to elapse. Yet that is all I ever wanted. That, and this intimate look.

THE COMPASS ROOM

Each book has a title and all chapters have numbers and each page has a number and each paragraph begins with a clear indentation, a pause or a clearing of a throat, and each sentence ends with a period and each word ends with a sound and each time we meet has the allure of progress away from something medieval such as violent unpaved roads and bawdy unplucked fowl running amok in the uncleared fields at the outer regions of fiefdoms. We congregate in dinners that are literate and referential, to books, to other people, to friends who favor not being there, knowing that we will speak about them lovingly yet with candor, sudden intonations of confession, unfounded opinions, half-truths, to oblige their spirits and to position ourselves nicely for the future, carving out trenches and borderlines that can be bent later, but not broken, when we ourselves choose to be absent. The noise of the news comes over the radio while someone has put a tape on the stereo, fusing a concert of musical effort and topical events beneath the chop chop of the vegetables and the scraping of nerves which run along the legs of chairs and pass into the doorbell, ringing as we all arrive.

We are all in love. Or we wouldn't be friends. At some point we have each of us pressed earnest notes into soaked winter pockets, or sat on the porches of houses at the latest hours of evening, leaning back into shadows and sharing a cigarette while someone who should be listening is asleep. Their absence wraps itself in the smoke or in the space between stairs, and a touch from a hand to a knee registers in the silence and brain as the slide of a mallet along the grooves of a gong. Bumping knees call to eyes that look away and suddenly wish for interruption, to be tucked back safely into any other night, reading a half-awake novel in a body-scented bed; the other person moving in and out closing up the various entrances to the house. Suddenly with one nudge of bare leg against leg, the danger of not living in a single obligation rushes out of the flesh in a frenzied take-off of mental flight. Until one of us visualizes pulling the elbow of the other for the effect of unbalancing our moral positions, toppling our lips onto each other, forging a necessity of hands and waists in the awkward, tipped-backward edge of passion. And one of us imagines pressing the other back across the damp wood of the porch to spread your gorgeous hair against an actual surface rather than the space between us. You smell like wine. And the next week we are still unable to stop touching accidentally at our places around the table, through the candles burning uselessly in too much electric light. The pleasure of cooking a large dinner for many people is that the ingredients fold into the recipe and the baking timer rings at the end. Never again will containers of flour, boxes of brown sugar, shakers of paprika be considered separately when we assimilate to the meal.

They were wrong.

The world feels flat. A compass plate cuts diametrically through a ball. Pinned in the center. Step toward anything and the world tilts rather dizzyingly downward — sloping to the edge of a cheap game-board, almost dumping the contents. Even thinking about moving tips the thin cardboard world, as words cluster into an intention, causing desire to gather on one side of the mind, just behind the eyes, and then as though pulled by a magnet, the weight of rain — the whole plate topples, slides off-balance and whoa! you slip toward the edge, scrambling back to the center, take my hand, stand on either side of the tiny pyramid swivel. Jump over the needle. Don't look at her. Don't ask about him. Don't think my name. Or imagine the topology of a full plate, mountains of potatoes, rivers of juice, balanced perfectly on a finger. Hungry? Be forewarned, hunger is heavy. Escape to the end of the earth. Don't let your eyes fall to the ground. Carry your thoughts in empty hands. Leave. Don't put your back into anything. Put the idea down slowly and only when you've balanced it with something else.

They were wrong.

Days don't end. Again I say something and you say it's all the same. A stone is dropped in the pool which ripples evenly to all sides; there are no natural corners. We're all stuck in artificial timezones. The sun drops and slides across the horizon, begging on its knees and stands up on the other side toward the mountains. It never disappears. Don't bother speaking, it's all one long day around here. C visits T, reacts to G, leaves A. Nothing changes. The chessboard tilts wildly, just don't move your pieces. Pawn. Knight. Race you to the edge. Knight for Rook. Rook takes Pawn. First to the edge becomes a Queen. Where were we when this began? The sun passes overhead and kneels down again, crossing and standing. Just grab any one of us in the dark, when the dark season comes, we all know these arctic winters. Line up the pieces. Stare for hours at the board and picture each move. Then look up and play it to the end.

They were wrong.

You can't walk alone. Bears don't want to hurt you, but they will if you surprise them. Talking to yourself is absolutely necessary. Or singing. Bells on the shoes help. T promised C, but G got jealous and angry at A. It'll follow us to the grave. I said that to myself, I said. I heard myself thinking, I thought. What did you say, I thought? I thought so, I say. I say, I said. I thought I'd say so, I thought. I'd say I thought so, I thought I'd say. I'll say, I think. I think not, I say. The bells on the shoes think so too. You can't walk alone because we love you too much. You can't walk alone because you think you are and the bears think not.

We were young when we lay in bed pretending to sleep. New theories came along threatening everything. G claims credit for the idea, but really we all invented him: the Perfect Burglar. Announcing: "the abolition of the separating function of the wall." We had sleep-overs as an excuse, daring each other to spend five, ten minutes in the attics or crawl spaces. Coming back to the group was a relief, and the reward was telling, with only slight exaggeration, the horrible things that happened when we were alone. Once we told a really terrifying Burglar story, sent C and A to the attic, locked them in and turning off all the lights, snuck downstairs. They scared themselves so badly they couldn't stop crying and G's mother had to call their parents to take them home. "We are returning to an honesty of thought and feeling in a land aching for mass-producible dwellings." The Burglar was our hero, despised and feared and awesome. Well, what with desire, generally. We reveled in the panic. Yelling bloody murder. Male and female blended in fearful stomp-stepping on the couch, running around the furniture. We ended together, huddled under tables, hiding under blankets, half-laughing children wooed by feeding, the homologous behavior of birds, where passing half-digested food beak to beak becomes a sign of prowess, of the ability to serve and protect; the first kiss. We waited fearfully in the nests. Function is beautiful; we fall in love with the things that save us. Feed me with your mouth. If a burglar comes in, we reasoned, he wants to steal things, probably to feed his family, he doesn't want to hurt anyone, that only happens when someone unexpectedly catches him. We stayed under the blanket trying to understand. If the Burglar hurts people, he's forced to; he'd much rather escape. It's our fault if he's caught in the Act. The new buildings blend construction and material: the clouds on the reflecting windows, the open rooms, flat domicile roofs. Using housetops for gardens gives an improved view to billions of passengers in the air. So obviously, pretend to be asleep during the whole thing. Let the burglar do his business and leave. The problem was, and we were advanced in our reasoning: to pretend to sleep, you have to actually stay awake, or risk waking up for real, accidentally, from being really asleep where you forgot to pretend. Years later, changes would be summed up by silly, ornamental things: a haircut, a wedding ring, crutches, glasses, new clothes, a slight attitude. But the modern architecture makes no discrimination between walls and windows. Between rooms. Between inside and outside. What's mine is yours. We knew each other's childhood homes by heart. How could we know that the abolition of the separating function means that support beams and foundations are exposed: Glass. Steel. Natural light. Nothing from the pebbly surface of the earth to obstruct the sun. Once the conventions were understood, any of us could tell a Burglar story with equal force. We practiced cooperating with all he asked for, in case we did forget and fell fast asleep — *whatever you want, take this, take me for ransom*. Neighbors pass by and in passing are let in. The home is a small cell in the larger unit, the street. We agree to pretend sleeping until further notice. We test one another. But flesh is often weak. Flying in bombers over their homeland toward the front, pilots get sleepy in the dark without special training.

The door is open. The light is on. For you this is an invitation. A familiar voice sings: "Come in!" Here, you are welcome. Did someone say "come in"? No, it was your imagination. You merely had to look at the building, the room, the space left open for you. Something in your mind tells you what you can and can't do. Here, it must be safe to come inside because the architecture is so comforting. Or might an inkling of danger lurk in open places? Nah. Come right to the heart of things; the room at the center of rooms where there is a door on each wall and light pours in from all directions. That's right: doors are open, lights are on. Four walls produce four corners and the light coming from the next room pulls your eyes through the doorway. You sit on a perfectly sturdy chair. The door nearest you is swung open so far that the doorframe is entirely visible. This might make you feel even better. The door on the far wall is only open halfway. Hmm. The lights in the next room are brighter than those in this room. The lights in this room come from two sources: the ceiling, the lamp. The ceiling light is a circular tube of fluorescent gas. The lamp light is a bulb. One has a switch and one has a cord. One is for you and one is for me. We each have a light to turn off and on. At the moment, we both have our lights on. This is perfectly pleasant. I doubt we would both turn our lights off. It doesn't seem to be in the cards. Two people can play some games while four people can play most of them. We should wait for the others to arrive. For us the lights are on and the doors are open. Nothing hiding in here. Nothing hidden. The lights in the next room are even brighter so if we tried to hide something we couldn't do it there either. And finally there's the outside. Bright, dazzling *out*-of-doors, framed in a corridor of doorways. People with things to hide don't sit in lit rooms with doors wide open. That's how we know we are safe. From ourselves and from each other. Safety in numbers, and if you don't have numbers . . . What? You're surprised that I've switched off my light? It's just for fun. I just wanted to see how much darker the room would get without it. Added a grain or two of darkness. And the room next door looks even brighter. The light from your lamp looks stronger; it resists the darkness more. There, I'll turn mine back on. Better? I get up to swing one door closed. No! you yell. No need to yell, I was just joking. I just wanted to see what would happen if one of the doors were closed. How would we feel in here then — a little asymmetrical? a little claustrophobic? A little unsafe? What if we started doing things that nobody could see . . . what dangers lie in that? There, I'll open the door again. Now all the lights are back on and the doors are open. So what is there to do? Shall we talk? Of course we can always talk. But what about the sound traveling? Right, we'll only say things that can travel anywhere. Diplomatic expressions. And we'll only sit where the rest can see us. In the light, bright open room. The lights show nothing happening and no secrets. We sure are safe in here. From ourselves, from whatever. Dangerous things don't hide in these rooms because they would be exposed immediately. No, you say, don't turn off both lights. What? Maybe just for a minute?

The crashed car's wheels look heavy but somehow keep turning stubbornly on the wrong course. C came to meet her at the plaza for coffee, to try to settle what he meant when he said he thought they were meant to be together. Then they heard metal scraping, saw the car flipping. C rushed forward. Don't mess with the scene, G warned. Adobe walls crumble if they're not maintained. She quotes his words back to him. Certain substances add moisture and certain remove it. Where the world is made from dirt, the witness scratches the surface only to reveal layers of undifferentiated versions. The dry dirt-built houses are exotic and the horizon is enormous. Your skin has taken a permanent tan, she remarks, to blend in, as though I'd never seen you pale, cold, talkative. You can disagree, you can back away, but you can't deny the witness the scene. Arroyos are dry for long stretches of winter. And desert night pours thick black paint over the scattered halting of things. The temperature drops. The darkness dries dull to gray. At dawn, the sky is a closed eyelid, painted peach and licked smooth. Meanwhile, during cross-examination, a specialist demonstrates how simultaneous equations are best calculated by organic material in liquid solutions. Kiss me inappropriately, she'd begged after a few margaritas. Rescue vehicles converge at the plaza and people run forth with blankets; others escape the traffic.

The overturned car wheels continue vainly; an ongoing thought. Mechanically, the force is acting on the axle, dividing the direction of 'forward' into opposing points, causing ongoing circular movement. Chemically, witnesses save themselves first. G came to see C after two years of saying, *remember the rainy climate, decaying leaves.* There are no trees here, was the first thing she'd noticed.

They are approached by a policeman who wants information. My plane is in an hour, G says, I don't have time to stand around and explain. Ask him, she pushes C forward, he was here, though he'll try to deny it. Dust flies from their boots. Sacred earth drinks down blood and thousands of prayers, and returns few favors. You think I will always come back, G says quietly.

C walks G to the bus. Look, the car wheels, — they repeat it as though by recognizing the same thing they're finally communicating. Boots don't leave prints in the dust unless a little water has recently been present. The air is afraid to add friction to anything. The danger of water is on hunger not thirst. There is a layer of forgetfulness on the plaza, drowsy sunburnt hues, while the so-called Martyrs overlook their crimes from monuments on the highest ground. There's no natural shade in this town, few clouds, the light leaves little to wonder about. Light is the liquid drowning us, in which we calculate impossible sequences. The body is the blueprint of all technology: our eyes, cameras; our proteins slosh around as multitudinous mega-computers. We wrote endless theories about "probability," now behind us. The plane over Los Alamos at night flies in a grid and, noiseless, can only be seen if you know what you're looking for. The passengers have been cut through the crumpled doors. Heavy car wheels roll on the sky without tread or traction. Some accidents choose us. What if we reached out and tampered with them? I guess we'll never know what could've happened, G says, throwing her suitcase in the belly of the bus. From her seat she watches C approach the car. He's going to interfere, she thinks, amazed. And arching his fingers back he opens his palm and presses the tire in the canyon between finger and thumb.

You say that you will suddenly appear. That if I call, you're here. You promise to grab me, hold me so tight. Remember, you said, you want this as much as I do. Remember, I said, you don't know me, you said it's better that way. You can't hide if you try, you tell me. You say you'll find me, you won't ring the doorbell, that would ruin the surprise. We are meant to be together, you say. You'll whisper through the door and I'll know. You'll be taller than a woman, your chest will be harder, your lips harder, your eyes harder, but I will melt them, as you've said I've done to your iron willpower. You promise your shadow across the doorway, the strength of your hand on the knob. You will come by plane and bus and train. You will come over the hills marching singlefile, closing in, closing ranks. Down the center of the highways. You said you will come by sea and air and land. You will come in uniform, or in broad daylight. You will grab me, squeeze me, press yourself into me, you can't wait, the wait is making you crazy. You have said how much you love me. How nothing else matters. Someday there will be nothing to explain. You will lift me when you see me, from behind, when I've almost forgotten to think of you. In this town are only a few exits, the houses detached and blinds in the windows guaranteed by law. Some houses are shingled an awful mix of colors, some are aluminum-sided and stay brighter in the diffused light. There is cement around each house and little grass. Some of the streets are so flat and hard it's like walking on a game board covered with plastic pieces. Green pieces, pink pieces. Against the brown cardboard sky. Pieces may be missing but this town is too small to become lost in. A town that should have burned when history was burning cities a century ago. Now it is stuck without ashes to rise from.

In the mornings the streets are deserted. By evening, the streets are deserted. She fumbles with keys at her backdoor in the dark. The key doesn't turn, she leans in, her fingers raw and stinging from pressing the sharp object, from trying to force it to do what it won't do. Open, open the door. Perhaps I will jump out of a closet to scare you. If I can get inside quickly, without your seeing, perhaps I'll pretend I'm not home. You hide outside the door, holding your breath. You'll climb the back stairs slowly, keeping the lights off. You have never been here. What will I be waiting with? Sharp, long scissors just for fun, a gun? You say there is only one thing you want. You are hard and your sweat is hard. You are scared of what you might feel for me. Scared I'm prepared for you. You are unsure you can really own up to your promises. You said you'd show me new things. You are still the boy with dreams. You are still the boy across the alley. You will arrive at the airport, circling in a thousand planes. The parking lot is full of your cars. You will arrive at the train station from all directions, come down with the rain, tossed to my door wrapped in newsprint. You sprout from the flowerpots, clog up the drains. Delivery trucks will dump you off in gross; you'll flow through the hurricane barrier with storms. Rise in bread, sit out with the mail, talk through the dialtone on the telephone. She believed him when he promised to come see her. He is going to come see me, she told everyone. I don't know when. Some of the streets are one-way, but one way or another he'll find me. He spoke to her once as an ordinary man, a friend. Does that mean he speaks for all men? The arrival of his words cannot match his arrival. He will approach as she is fumbling for her keys. A, T, G, C. We promise to be there.

T was arrested for taking a long blue police barricade that said,

police line — do not cross

G had asked him to take it and so she considered herself responsible. She would give anything for that responsibility, as it was the first time she'd asked him for something. When police chased them from the park at four in the morning, now that, she conceded, was T's fault. Many other things they got in trouble for were C's fault: cutting school, leaving wine half-full in the closet. But stealing signs was exclusively her idea, each one of them, except a plaque T brought her once, unexpectedly. "Now that," she confided to C in the hall between classes, "is a sign."

Yield

Stop

G wrote poems first, she didn't know where that idea came from. They were purposively impossible to understand. She meant something direct by them, but transmitted it scrambled. Poetry, she thought, is top-secret arsenal. Then the gangs started doing it. Encryption became all the rage. She wrote in her small blue book crossing out every fourth word, reversed the phrases, and then copied the remaining words into a note, slipped in the grooves in T's locker. We sat in the long spring grass and planned all the places we would go. C and T rough-housed and landed in a pile. There was no code-breaking in less than 10^{20} operations. Just the four of us, for starters, made too many combinations. A and T were dating at the time, so G got T to steal signs that pleased her. She gave explicit directions: exactly which corner a sign was on, exactly what time to unscrew it. The crimes were meaningless, benefiting no one. The orders were clear. Nothing could be clearer.

One way

And of course the most prized were those printed in white on green with the names or the numbers of the streets where we all lived.

56th	*50th*	*49th*	*(& a shopping cart)*
Greenwood		*Kimbark*	*Woodlawn*
(& orange highway cones)		*47th*	*Ellis*

The whole neighborhood lay downturned in the unmowed grass, torn up sentences in the laps of dandelions. So when the police caught him taking the barricade, she was outraged that they didn't arrest her, but possession is one-hundred percent of the crime and she hadn't possessed any of it.

Some movie recently shot at the lodge has us all laughing at the possibilities for horror — *redruM* or rather *gniddeW* on the mirrors:

A: "This could be us."

G drops the embrace. A's dress stands white against snow, her new husband's sleeve just inches from this startling phrase. G wonders about A's skin under the lace, whether the mysterious discolorings have been resolved. A few feet between the glacier on one side, and the audience, the wind steals their handmade vows. They lean closer to the mike; she narrates a private excursion. Our drive up here today, minister and maids, white and gray, all who came, stand for ceremony's sake.

Dinner comes to circular tables and of course we surround her; friends from childhood don't get ignored at these occasions, representing what will soon disappear.

At some point, A mentions she is moving to Japan and that the meal is macrobiotic, or the other way around. In the throes of fading lime-light, G runs into the kitchen. Eyes stay by the door until she returns, reporting boiling water controlled by the height of flame, turned down as the foam crawls over the lip. Yes, the hens were fed organically and killed painlessly and G saw for herself vegetables sliced and arranged toward beauty, not just functional feeding. This was the way A taught G to cook years ago, when her skin began manifesting mysteries. Specialist after specialist shrugged. So A took health into her hands and eating became the antidote, the control, and G her partner, sleeping over, studying the effects of what goes in and what comes out, together; how to balance the essential properties of food and by extension, all things, and each other. Balance the plate with opposite colors, not all green, not all yellow, and the right proportions of beans and grains. A wheel with two poles: salt and sugar, flower and root, and all that grows between them. Years later, G still remembers some recipes, and returning to the table makes statements about commitment and cooking. Her voice is too loud. Her face flushes. We all understand.

At dinner we're facing inward, giant arms coiling from the table, feeding the central mouth, common internal organs that intake and excrete and press tissue together, sharing functions. When one of us breaks away and floats toward the mountain, another one reaches through their place to grab more, as though each bite were a footstep on the glacier. From inside the candlelit dining hall we can't see the darkness, the mountain skies dribbling snow onto black gravel so that one person slipping and falling on another for support during the walk, getting lost, reveals another in their place. Any part of a starfish survives, she knows the secret semi-colons, searching fragments always freefloating. G whispers naughty thoughts to us in the hot tub after the couple has gone: *That could be us? Does his arm over her shoulder feel like any similar weight?*

Bliss-waves alternate with troughs of turmoil, anguish, and relief. G froze the chains to make them colder on A's wrists, harder to resist. G put the chair in the middle of the room and pulled all the rest of the furniture away. They don't speak casually on this kind of afternoon. The silk scarves bind A's ankles and press her eyes, joining flight and fancy, in a studied school together. "Erotic experience linked with reality waits upon chance, upon a particular person and favorable circumstances." G laughs. Without warning she dribbles some heavy cream between A's thighs and chooses not to lick it off though she loves sweet and sour. Discontinuity is the pleasure. They see each other in flashes, like lightning in a doorway; blazing whites and impenetrable grays. A finger finds a groove along her labia shhhh! to keep her in place and straddle the chair, her left breast just an inch from her mouth. She can feel but not see her. They laugh. G leans forward and bites her nipple which is gathering toward her, she could again but she won't because no one has said so. "Onlookers briefly experience continuity when witnessing the long final exhalation of one who no longer has pauses between heartbeats." A steady beat allows no silence, no words form, and as accidentally her lips touch her neck, she is pinched hard, gasps and falls over the chair backward, freeing her hands, laughing again, unbroken laughter preventing dialogue, and this failed scene turns into a rehearsal, a composite of struggle, as discontinuous as their visits, their suffering which becomes the claim ticket for *hearts checked out from the library of emotional eroticism*. Calming, she tells her to begin speaking, still blindfolded she spins a fictional self; G asks routine questions, playing it cool, and A lets a finger drag across her wet cotton panties. G plays it nervous, like a virgin, not a lifelong friend. Love is a door into existence: love may be doomed but the door is not. Random objects are drawn into the doorway, creating a path, sometimes more like its opposite. G takes the blindfold off and her eyes are fiery, she can feel A shrinking from her, afraid to apply this past the threshold of afternoon. "Erotic passion without possession makes a transparency with another human being with whom to suffer isolation." In liquid they can finally dissolve. The ice is cold along her cunt, and burns where she quickly pushes in her tongue. Here they exit in the fluid elysium, where their bodies return to fundamental percentages. They insist they're detached, but their bodies do not finally believe their individual identities and go to water. G pushes herself into her erotic luck, numbers flash in her mind, they melt, the entire population of continents. They've devised codes to seal these afternoons, rooms to make sense of, objects to bring. A does as G instructs, instruction is the first response. Later, the pain comes from inside the throat when they speak. Come into my house and let me serve you. What do you like? The shadows in the doorways taste like peppermint and olive oil.

"Be happy, you who are leaving." For the airport. There is dark mist, no sky, the taxi's light goes on when the door is opened. The trunk has a light when it is opened.

The FDR is blue lit, the tunnels passages of rose. G lectured on Aristotle yesterday in class. By 96th street, the evaporation of the dew has left a powder-blue sky. The moon is alone with the dog star over the Triboro — whose cords makes her think of Odradek.

Another hot spot of red light at the toll. The driver has to flip on the ceiling light for her to pull some dollars from her wallet. Pray, pray, he will not speak to me, she thinks, I want to leave without saying anything more than, "*LaGuardia.*"

"The female differs from the male body as less differs from more." "Characters in tragedies are defined only by their actions." The cab window is permanently half-open and drizzle adds soot to the sky and to the glass. Pale smudged blue over the orange mecca of airport and the green splashes of signs listing airlines. G wishes she were coming back already.

But Baubo lifted her skirt and showed her sacred mouth and laughed and told dirty jokes. G tries again to push the chipped handle forward and close the window. She should not be flying in this condition.

"The male provides the form and the principle of motion." The pre-dawn breeze pushes wet fingers through her hair, touching the skin behind her ears, holding her cheeks in cool palms. Streetlight after streetlight blend the highway into the terminal. The female component is a residue of the future. "The female have the principle of cold." She says, "*United, please.*"

G's body needs to be explored in detail, lovingly, after the steel and plastic instruments of the doctor. T is going to pick her up. He promised to be gentle. Still, it is significant who is traveling. These maneuvers are not arbitrary. Beauty does not remain attached to bodies but rises and gets caught in objects at higher levels. Under the overhang the light is good enough for the porter to slip the correct tags on the luggage. She lets him carry the bags because she doesn't want to waste saying, "No."

Women lack vital heat which weakens their cooking, causing a residue of blood which pulls out each month like the waxed paper in cereal boxes. G hadn't called him for a long time, and T must have found out her diagnosis from one of the others. He phoned immediately with instructions on where to pick up the tickets.

Inside the airport there is only light, not a single shadow to be found. G has an hour to wait before the flight and she closes her eyes, still picturing the gate number and the empty waiting area. There is no difference between seeing and having seen. That is why children resemble parents as doctors are to patients. As airports are to times of day. As blood is to libraries. Only the military operates airports in the dark of night — vampire maneuvers.

It was a source of pride that we managed to get together without the others for many years, through both our marriages. I loved how her fingers aged tough and I took them as we kissed hello, weaving mine in, not letting on that we'd just spent another weekend recently, though G eyed me suspiciously, squeezed my ass and handed me groceries.

During dinner we gave relaxed, funny accounts of our summers. The waves plunged into the blue-night beach until A announced her pregnancy. Silence broke across the table as though we could each take credit.

You didn't even ask me, I accused her later.

He won't want any part of it, A reaching for my arm, the marsh reeds bending to the ground, trying to touch me. Her hood hides half her face. Gale force, I imagine. This is hurricane country.

I thought you'd ask me, I whined, waves plunging, her smile holding steady.

T and I have talked about it for years, she topped the surf, you aren't the only one with the right parts. A laugh; anyway he doesn't want to raise a kid. He doesn't have a steady job or a steady boyfriend. Her logic eroding.

I knew when she'd asked me about this, years ago in some desert when we were way too young; she shouldn't have been listening then. Now, the saltless taste of aging tears.

I'm excited to do it alone, turning her back into the gusting spray, spinning in the storm. You'll be a godparent, uncle, anything you want. Again a plunging smile.

I didn't want to hear when they'd done it: I drank half a bottle of tequila and went upstairs. T came up and slipped under the covers, put his arms around me, told me he was so sorry: of course he'd assumed she'd told me. I kissed him deeply, drunk, we slowly fucked. I love you, he whispered, and I love him too. I realized nothing was more enduring than that. We sat up and I expressed concerns for the baby and he told me I was really being a pig.

So when can I see you? I asked as we all lay reading. Whenever, she smiled casually. G and T took her dog for a walk. The ocean had changed glassy and clear and I crawled over and lay next to her on the daybed, reaching for her belly, visiting already.

Once a man came into G's house; excuse me, but it needs to be said: this man was not our type. He was her mother's idea. Luckily, friends say things as they see them.

For years G's mother wanted a "Man." There is no arguing that that's what he was. He was introduced this way, his smell was of a Man, her mother said "Man" on the phone to her friends. Her mother cupped "Man" and blew on it for luck. Shaking the ivory sticks back into the cardboard box, she bet with herself. She lit candles. She knew a man from his facial hair, the patterns of baldness, the smell on his hands. She knew a man because he could pull at any arm and it couldn't pull away. Her mother burned sweet smelling sticks until the house stank. His design was that of a Man, man-made man parts, she winked. She told herself he was a good Man, implying the opposite, accentuating the positive. Manna. Her mother burned more candles. Men like ambiance, they like to look through smoke. They don't want noise. The plates he ate off became news. She knew a Man from the silence he trailed, and like a kitten she wanted to tackle and unwind it. She had many theories about Men, and she induced observations to test them. How Men are and how they can be haunted. This tussling was part of a Man's organic system. Her frame was bony though she made her house enormous for him. Arms in places are thin and bones can break just by squeezing them. Mannequin: a life-size or partial representation of the human body used to display clothes. He made ugly noises at her mother, ugly sounds into her, she whispered "wild" on the telephone to her friends. She applied home economics to the bedroom, kitchen, garage and basement, each coded for certain appliances, the air ionized toward "his" or "her" things. She applied science to her eyes, her lips, but not like her mother, dripping it between her legs with a wand attached to the shower. She went back to school to learn to speak so he would hear her and to maybe become someone he would hire. She cooked up meals that could never be leftover. Man became her mantra. His lips formed ugly shapes as he ate and later in his half-mumbling sleep his jumping lids made her pull back, a mannered fright. But her mother was so glad to have him in her house, she placed his long-stem roses like bars in the windows. "His" was an ugly monogram, "He" a sacred pronoun pulling the life from creatures, stuffing their skins into cereal boxes stuffed in the freezer, the little house began filling with bloodless bodies. She fell back, palms up. Excuse me, she said in laughter *manqué* as he walked up and down the stairs. She was becoming all eyes. And as he grew to squeeze out the size of the house, all eyes were cast upon him, barnacled to his shirt and hanging from his lips, one for each look cast until there were millions there, each with a dry-rimmed crater.

There was no wedding because A refused, and then we all refused to go.

The sides of a square.
The points of a cross.
The cardinal directions.
The most who can play scrabble.
The primary winds.
The horsemen of the apocalypse.
The chambers of the heart.
The seasons.
The railroads in monopoly.
The elements.
The leafs on a lucky clover.
The chemical units of DNA.
The temperaments.
The suits of cards.
The rivers in paradise.
The Evangelists.
The stomachs of a cow.
The quarters in a dollar.
The stages of life.
The essential humours.
The streets around a block.
The score and seven years ago.
The prophets.
The letters in the name of God.

The balls to walk.
The gates.
The basic food groups.
The legendary mountains.
The legendary kings.
The Alcott girls.
The walls of a room.
The downs in football.
The irreducible factors of sensation.
The accepted dimensions.
The ethical "cords."
The legs on a chair.
The great vows.
The parsley, sage, rosemary, and thyme.
The noble truths.
The outdated ways of life.
The product of two and two or four and one.
The primary colors.
The world-trees.
The legs of a dog.
The minimum number of people to make a party.
The hands in bridge.
The causalities.
The corners of the earth.

My spine, T confessed, *is injured in many places (ways) at once; I can bare-ly move, the pain, the pressure on the nerves. I won't be able to see you.* The let-ter is written in pencil and barely legible, the lead so soft it's been eaten by the page.

The chollas have flowered but some pieces, broken-off, lie around as skeletons. The cactus flesh dries away and decays, leaving honey-combed carcasses. The spine inflames. Liquid tubes of fire. *Maybe the fluid should be surgically drained,* C suggests. *In your letter, you speak of the injury as though it's some retribution, a price for having too much fun when we were younger. How can you say that? p.s. I can still come see you, please write back immediately.* A spine hardly needs defining unless you don't have one. A spindle is responsible for moving organic material to opposite ends of the cell. The nerve tract, longitudinal, connects the brain and the mus-cles. Organic matter is subject to deterioration. In the meantime, the canal protects the energy. In the meantime, C waits, his flesh weak, and the white matter, ascending and descending, can't adequately surround the gray.

In a packet of letters age can be determined by the repetitions of cer-tain words; C knows many of T's stack up ring upon ring. C tries writ-ing about this and rips it up. Nerves bypass the brain when flooded and cause a reflex. But C has other strengths: the way his quiet arms twine into resiliency. Something about the delayed effects of rough-housing. Something about canceling each other too often. Spines are also leaves reduced to a point, as a matter of protection against predation. The short cholla stick, hollow and light, a souvenir of the desert, a twirl of petrified chromosome, separated from the cell.

My spine injury makes it impossible to walk (the drugs make it impossible to talk) T writes back, and he offers to show C a broken series of bones running from his head, twenty-six. Attached painfully to muscles, vertebrae support the whole body, becoming larger and stronger toward the weight-bearing places, but fading like an alphabet with age. The cholla flower yellows early in the season, a sprawling desert hand reaching toward heat where it passes. The flowers are hard bundles, not really petals. Muscles. Long and narrow with tapered ends. They work the ten-drilled body. Some bones are stationary and some moveable so that contractions pull one toward the other. C cancels his plane ticket and stacks the letter with the others in a dry, safe place. All skeletal muscles are under the voluntary control of the nervous system. When pain shoots through you have to move, it's the only relief; and to make some noise. *I've injured my spine, I can't walk (talk) and by the way . . . and by the way . . .* The heart is not attached to bone or controlled by motor nerves, allowing it to continue without the aid of these systems when they fail.

It all started (as most things do) with a set of two (two sides) a front and a back (a top and bottom) — the basic unit (the smallest combination which can provide the illusion of motion.) One side painted with one image (a beautiful bird.) The other side is painted too (though not necessarily with:) a Cage, dark bold strokes with a wide brush. Then thread a line through the grommet, and crank or spin the contraption from the string. Around and around (Bird) Cage (Bird) Cage fast, faster, spin! Cage (Bird) Cage (Bird) — at the proper speed the two images blend (so that the Bird, once sprawled on its empty space is caught inside the opposing Cage.) The children tire easily of any two things, and must have more, so long as their nickels stay solid. Rowboat (Dinosaur) Rowboat (Dinosaur). Try it at home. Well, eventually the show had to move on as the apparatus wound down and the images pulled back to their separate sides. When accustomed from the beginning with something as children are, they can't imagine life without it. And so the medium was perfected through the century.

We survive on the persistence of collective vision. Given separate accommodations from birth for sleeping — we wake alone. But during the ensuing days in a circular white room we mark off spaces. For long hours we work on separate pieces, then proudly step into the viewing room, behind walls and watch through slots carved down from the ceiling. The show spins like a drum (we all know the basics of the medium by now) and our eyes mete out the motion (holding to one thing until replacing it with another) — blending our work together. We kept it simple: black and white, one action over and over (for example: coming and going through a door, a figure appears to walk, jerkily, clumsily). Stepping through. Stepping back. A group show which friends never finish, paralyzed as we are by the vision of its persistence. The zoetrope didn't last long before someone figured out how to project light through it. Oh, the first audiences may have been amazed (while we are jaded and see that nothing goes anywhere in an illusion.) Historically these halting attempts mostly interested immigrants and children, and a hundred years later, a mirrored column rises in the center of the room and leaves the simple action reflecting there.

T shows us blueprints slashed in red ink. He failed drafting by design-ing a library with room for only one book & a hotel with no windows. We laugh approvingly. He laughs too. T is relieved to get away from school, though he seems distant, as if somehow we caused him the prob-lems for which we now comfort him. C forgot to tell G that T would be joining us & she went upstairs when he arrived & he didn't follow. The afternoon weather changed so we collected long metallic feathers by the lake. A's parents are away, she whispers to me, "I can't believe it still matters." Though tripled in age, we run amok in their house; teenagers dying to fulfill some destiny. We draw the feathers through our fists. C comes up kissing G from behind, asking forgiveness, slipping his hand to her stomach, causing me to roll newspapers for a fire. She turns in his arms and forgives him. T spreads blueprints around the house. Feathers touched too much tear from their spines, separating where they didn't at first seem to have parts. We lean in around the table as T sketches. I dub it all "Maybe Space"; buildings grow & age, get hurt or sick or unravel along with us; an architecture of living materials:

Doorknobs soften into tumors, detach and float up the walls out of reach. The driveway squirms if touched by car wheels. A garden erupts and caves into a pool. Or jump off a polished cliff, the only way into the bedroom. On humid days the house sweats maps: red and blue until one of us gets up to leave, when dishes whiz up the trees on toy train tracks. Windows are too high to see through or else they're cut in the floor, a view of the ground. After each meal computers celebrate their jelly, oozing across tile, hardwood, stained-brick, now sand, floors. When you come home the house consists only of a long, cushioned window seat. When I leave, bookshelves trail like toilet paper from my heel. When C gets angry, the roof slides back and forms a gallows from the hillside. The stairs turn to marble with red silk carpets sliding down them like nightgowns off a shoulder we all scramble up, after each other, in icy boots. The house shyly disappears the more we think about it.

The weekend passes slowly. We take turns at the t-square, ruler, compass, staying up all night. At some point T announces his return to school, recommitted now to standard angles. I flop beside A in her parent's room, our voices muted by the bedspread, mirrored doors half-open to closets of colored clothes hanging dark together. It's the same scene, me kissing her, she leads my hands down her warm skin. The feather, without the wing, loses its protective oils & ages rapidly. She & I share a grip on one as hands curve with seamless thighs, until the music bangs on the floor & she sits up. The portraits along the stairs go blank as silently with downturned eyes we emerge & A pulls T from his chair & leads him outside through the back door. I am caught on the landing dissolving so I grab my heart off it, blowing eraser crumbs away. Contingent houses are perfect dwellings for contingent communities unconcerned with trespassing or old-growth territory. Even the length of the drive from one place to another depends only on seasonal lapses and mottos of indifference. Sometimes it takes us ten years to find the house, sometimes just a few minutes.

The pictures came out beautifully.

In each the liquid is a devastating blue. Sun strikes the camera lens and sprays back across tabletops, knees, sunglasses.

For some reason, they're reclining in every photo. On the beach. On deck chairs. On pillows in the hotel. In one picture, they've constructed a little cabana in the sand out of t-shirts, towels, and driftwood. The liquid is dazzling. Someone reclines peacefully in an island of shade.

Halfway through the block of photos, they begin looking darker, sunburned, disheveled. The liquid is always the same burning blue. Did we have that many beautiful days?

I brought my camera, the only one of us who remembered. I also booked the hotel, rented the car, found out which dancing place was best for our particular combination of tastes. Kissing goodbye, splitting up toward separate gates at the airport, one of them whispered to me, "You were the perfect host."

I had oral sex several times during the week.

There are pictures of the cookout, of silver-skinned fish surrounded by vegetable-kabobs, thinly sliced steaks, corn burning on the grill. A feast of dark, juicy colors lit by flashbulb, with bonfire sidelight in orange.

By the end of the roll, I'd begun to take nostalgia shots: our row of stools at the clam-bar, the disco, the changing booths at the beach, us standing in groups, arms tight around some waists, looser over shoulders. Deep, satisfied smiles all around. The final *coup de grâce* is a panorama of overlapping shots from ankle-deep in waves turned back toward them.

I am still upset; "perfect host" stuck in my ear like salt water after a dive. That hotel was not my home. I didn't buy rounds of drinks. I was no one's hostess and the implications rob me of my pleasures, the choices of my trip. I had amazing sex one night on the beach. One afternoon behind the pool. Is that what that meant, that I served everyone? And who didn't?

I reach the bottom of the stack and tap them on the table, realizing that I am in every single picture: in their smiles, in the space between arms and bodies. I am in the foreground of every portrait, reflected in their faces, implicated in the angle of every shot. There is not a single photo of me, the one who remembered the camera.

WALKING

the longest journey is still

perstept

a bondage

    between a going foot

and the inertia
        that isn't
                more than a familiar environment
a stop
    a step
        even in the slowest rhythm
                  a stop
a step
a tempo so
    slow

it's a
    pause
a daydream thought without effect or fiddling with a key
for an ongoing entrance
                to the slightest smell   word
                  the shortest story
    ramparts rage

    in the going which is always
detaching landscape
              heading home for a promise
              a Ride, ultimately a desire
          meaning from here to there, an end

    and not the sort of meadows   trespassing
    the 19th century
    the "solitary walking mind"
    but the street fragments

    where one neighborhood

joins another
       an individual
       a perfect stranger
       in a gray parka with fur
       in passing   is replaced with some
       abstraction
       possibly a crowd
       but for now
take two steps in place to keep the stranger
always ahead

stale smell of cigarettes   on my person
travels with me, the taste in my throat   an atmosphere

a pause   a flag snap hitting the pole
the cutting   is successive
                  a payphone, exact change, no answer
                    phone cords dangle, snipped
     allow
              assertion and rumor
    perstept
step   turn   a performance of silence
                  I follow the stranger who seems to
                  go where I'm thinking
       the beginning

                  without speaking
each time again   a smell of dough
     a step breaks the lyric   steamed salt
     glance   tight fists, the magnolia buds
        step
step   a red bead necklace
                  in the thawing slush
always partially skips
the mind in steps   the tight-trope
        nothing innocent
             the white bouillon
             cubes of oil on the harbor

the baker strolls his cat on a piece of clothesline
so early I'm the only one who sees him
he

       is   my story
      concrete

                   paved
          interruptions flat cold-beverage cup
            benches pebbles   soiled mitten
       broken bottle held by half-peeled label
           soaked newspapers
         pizza box antifreeze phone books

              it's all

                         what I remember to call
the continuous discrete movement

                         my fifteenth birthday
          that is
a world that means rather than an earth that is
becoming   the scenery
a story junkpile use value medicinal herb garden
the observatory
basement windows grab passing ankles body parts in reflection

until I see a face I think shouldn't be there

and crossing into someone I remember we stand for a few moments staring
our steps stopped so that they're unrecognizable as such we stare and won-
der what we're each doing there..............................the territory of a walk
including and excluding thoughts of what should be and remarking upon
itself when it crosses back onto itself there is something humorless about
this girl I begin to think as my pulse slows because her name rhymes with
mine.....................the barrier that is broken is the fire that travels up our
hands as down a trail of leaves and burns out at the tongue

for how do I even remember my steps?

                       not the metaphoric kind
I feel that object   bronze babyshoe in my pocket

but the real ones
         that press
the earth
and the earth presses back
with equal force

which is hard to feel, if not comprehend entirely

broken cigarette   the earth pushes back

                    and so trying to remember even as I'm standing here
                              twisted plastic grocery bag
                                    the steps that brought me
                              half-buried in wet sand
                         to the earth that pushed me, as equally

                                             as I pushed

                    is hard because I don't think of steps like I should
                              some streets missing signs
                                    like hearing music
where
Anywhere I start

         I start
Anywhere I go

I go

                    there's no "generally speaking" as everything talks about itself

                    spilled detergent devil's claw and dandelion
                    angel's breath paper wadded with dog shit

the thirst is in the mouth of the morning
the rooms are private
in the grocery store we rarely find food we don't recognize
                    the broom tcccchk tccccchk
                              on the wet and dry sidewalk

somehow we speak of the beginning of the day
the same one word   skin
by one   blood relative
  by another   hospitality
 each expectation passes as it begins   plastic bag
the plot is hard to circumnavigate   can of soup
hard to see except in each of its steps   leather wallet
frames   blue windbreaker
each image   leaves mixed with
   each uneven patch of grass sand on the path
or sidewalk crack   syringes and latex
     fills in   my mother's apartment
and flows past   her boyfriend's
         Horizon
        why am I obliged to knock
an' I step   not to stay but to say something
an' I pause   it's been a long time, mother
an' I I think   you look like shit
  as I move   the excema seems worse
I think   the Horizon is running
  as I breathe   and I am a placeless creature
I think ahead
some words went wrong a wrong turn

         I am too young
some thoughts wandering   to drive for where you see
      something
passed description   how is care ever not needed
a garden hose waters the flowers
outside the store
         the past was easy
        the car window down
         motor on
all in the same breath   a cigarette poked through
  I vanish   the smoker kills himself
  when I walk   more slowly
habitually I mistake the bark for the dog

brown paper bags wet on the bottom
  break and spill
each distraction

creating a situation out of attention
comedy is forgetting a "goal"
which is the freedom of privilege

whereas   four tall kids
linked   across a fence

as a child is to her new mobility

                                        taking steps for granted

                        whereas

if I'd had balloons on my feet, I'd have noticed

if I'd had wheels or knives, I'd have noticed

if I'd never been able to move without the arm of another, I'd have
noticed
                        these gamboling spaces
as gifts
the dimensions of humans walking on earth
weight, duration, sound, stomping, pitch

stomping I remember   a person is created
                                where her involvement is

'cause stomping's a pleasure whose sound endures
in shock, up the leg into the hip
it makes a noise, and it's useful

and duration is the
                                coffee cup
                        erotic   erotic   erotic
            erotic   erotic   erotic   erotic
                        psychotic
                        sub-atomic

                              invisible strength that grows
                              radiant in time
                                        events sneak up
which is the pleasure of experience
why walking vanishes in the too common to notice
the mushrooms   wrapped in plastic

or there's our girl standing in the center aisle of a bustling supermarket
where I notice she doesn't understand the labels of the food, the swinging
placards, what's on sale *perstept* she is foreign and can't feed herself the
way she'd like, she must risk the tastes of foreign sauces and perhaps
parts of animals she is forbidden to eat, searching the bloody plastic for
the parts she euphemistically calls "meat" in her own idiom

forced patterns emerge in the faces on line at the register
"on line" implying that there is a line before we are all "in" it, that there
is something that we participate in before we even get "on it"
to this plate glass window or holding ice cream, the strange rotting bird-
wing, chicken

                                                        whatever

the ramp down snags the toe
and falling is a whole rigmarole
perhaps price per
perchance purchase
            perstept
where obviously mostly   I drop my bag
everyone is   a freshly laid trail of
"one foot in front of the other"   melting frozen food
involving every walker
the same way   a bus squeals its brakes
in everything   a bicycle swerves
and it's only the particular item
which is packaged differently

anything   that travels   the grass
has   once   along the
 continuities   meant   parking lot
 such as   travail   full of
 breathing and articulating   cat piss

because in the process of forgetting about walking, which is the "aver-
age" state of walking, the mind apportions the movement regularly, and
then totals and divides proportionately, so that we talk of "hitting one's
stride," hitting one's stride so that the walking measures "the intake of
things" against a common tempo, common to itself, things once invisible
in rhythm now so that I "see"

the way shadows drop from leaves

> that we are all
> nicheless beings

"headed" rather than "footing"

toward a promised Car, symbolic encasement and speed headlong into any
weather—unstoppable except in excess or malfunction—all external in the
speed—passing as viable as cinematography—the car's different legibili-
ty— insensitive touch—the nerve endings don't extend to the brain in
exactly the way the wind blows on the window—rather it's the eye though
the eye is a window and the feet pedals—there are levels that contain the
motion at different intervals—the car will have roads it can't make but fol-
lows—paved by consensus—one ways and social segregations of traffic,
Oh, when I get my license!—a different set of standards, though occasion-
ally the same like getting downtown on a birthday, the walker loves the car
for its journeying and ease, its speed — the roadsign pleasure of names and
directions and rules

> the smoker looks around
> for an ashtray, her cigarette
> tips & makes one from a shoe

very few cabs cruise these streets
the public bus tells it differently
mass-transit said something about more leisure time for the working
taking walking away from mass-migration too

> vagrancy is a walking slowed to the pace of poverty
> telling the story so slowly it is silenced

the public interest
these old houses of stained linoleum   careful gardens

for that matter is it possible to walk "backward," even if I'm turned
around, which I certainly have been, in both senses of the word, the first
of going in the "wrong" direction, wrong in that it is somehow not the
direction I "meant" to go, and the second of moving my body "at cross
purposes" to its design, the design of toes pointing in the direction of
"forward," rather than heels, which in the correct "wrong" sense, move
backward "toward" something, though mostly the mind is stuck with its
cross purpose and says that I am in this case moving "away"

So why this particular radio station blaring as I stand here, where it
has just rained

by all accounts

an average day

          whether this equals "an arithmetic mean"

or is "typical" of

          "purposeless" steps

an average day, like many others
                              now with guitar and a small amp
                              a burst of pigeons from the park

the bus took us away from the farmer
                    the farm a newly vacated landscape
          useless as a mountain   that winter-coat woman
is better off as tin cans
for a nickel each   to hold our meals
in the   somewhere of "there is a house
          needing   to be recognized"

                              as a garage the price is exorbitant

to reclaim territory

                           the stoops

                                  on this block

                                      have gates in front so as

                                              not to be confused with

seating

territory is the one thing that disappears when the subject disappears,
what's natural doesn't transcend itself in a useful intimacy
                                  extinction demolishes the world

let's drop that skin-encapsulated shit, science of pioneer virtues,
            simplicity, no nostalgia, no restoration of natural
            proportions   no reconnection with the   moral order
                  ahistorical recovery of asocial self

                  stepping into the stream each new time to remind them well
                  that some steps are more fucking equal than others

that the natural isn't "ah!" isn't the "ah, bucolic!"

                                in walking there are limits
        to road   recollections of personal and national and racial pasts
            acute moral apprehension, higher powers of expression
                  or there oughtta be

                              or my excitement makes the colors
            mute
a day marked
                            on the calendar, and going home
                            for the ride downtown

                          pause at a landmark
where one thousand women shoebinders and stitchers and five thousand
men shoeworkers marched through the streets of Lynn in a blizzard —
the shoe business came to a halt on Washington's Birthday 1860 and
through the snow through February through March into April they
walked on striking terrain where how and why one crossed the lines of

stepping & connected people into and out of stores all became a web of
tangled empty stomach pockets of emotion — an entire generation
walked without blurring their manifest intention
this landmark
reflects the concerted action of lining up the steps
in a decidedly American Way of walking
now in the right light one can still hear the faint circle
of shoebinders of women of a united story
steps striking one ahead, one behind

the sidewalk shakes as a fire-truck heaves up the hill

                                        a panacea of some same old
                                        vendors or vending machines
                                        dispensing historical dilemmas

the way yoghurt is not one thing but several communities
            as though
there weren't quotations from books

"Here Comes the Theme"   siren
the roving left-to-righter asks
"What on Earth is Happening Now?"   roving lights
the overdependence on the eyeball   polyphonic sirens
"Music need not be understood," but rather   spastic red off-on
"it must be heard" and replace   arhythmic lights
story for the word music
for the field happily blurs   blue police
                                                red firetruck lights
                                                blue on red the sky
                                                gray crushed aspirin

A birthday has no margins, the event arrives
flush with the curb
and the days are "occasions for experience"   people start looking
                                        differently at the garbage
                                            cans   the garage
                                        sniffing the air in case

something they think may have happened might make them
nauseous
but where pleasure has no purpose is it pleasure?

                                    the trucks surround the block
without answering
why something makes us go home or ever really want something
so bad you'll go through fire and hell to get a ride to it

a thought stops the sidewalk   the crowd turns inward
                                                swarms the house
                                                the bus driver pulls away
                                                without passengers

Story, they say
has
                        Direction
has that definite
                        Meaning
that is about meaning
and not about
                        Time
and
                        Going to a Job
that
                        Doing a Good Job means Getting There on
                                Time
and by the most
                        Scenic and Meaningful Route too

and being good company
a good
                        Character
and make sure it's
                        Clear
whywhywhy
                        that Story, they say

requires knowing the past and foreseeing the future
"feeling" where it's "going" each thing a useful and valuable
visible system of weather
where it doesn't matter about the reception
even the silent attention of a key in the ignition
is all the forecast calls for
nothing is open except the bakery
the baker trampling over where I   up
                                     step   to join him
                    on his threshold
to see what's the commotion   on Lewis Carroll's map
                                             on a scale of one to one
                                             so it can't be unfolded
in each thing its story

        a performance uniquely   not recognizing a particular house
                                                                     as home
a frame for experience
but where there's smoke

there is art
or nothing   each time out

no vantage "established"
or forced perspective
the world disaligns to any one pair of eyes
or any translation
in the witnessing of something burned but not burning
prioritizing the fixed and spatial, biographical
over the temporal fluid of sirens and birthdays
listening
                                     to the silence of smoke
speech flux   the not sizzling
bystanding
stop thinking   only one
        perstept   thought lingers in
trying to feel the motion   birds bouncing
and the weight   on the phone lines

at the same time   a promise of an end
new ideas   to a way downtown
continually   a mom trying to get
pop   out of the invisible
into view   dimensions
each step   which are promises
must remain   as eager as
responsive to   these looks of
pocks and coughs   strangers as
the "imperfections of the page"   the strapping men
always   in yellow rubber &
ready   yellow rubber boots
to shift   lined up along hoses
direction to   ax the windows   gas masks
space-time   ax down the garage door
embodying each other   oxygen tanks swim in
red   light

                    the fire truck headlights blink on and off
the ladder is part way   up a fireman stopped
carefully others swarm the garage the crowd quiets
and listens to the orders of the fireman into walkie-talkies
and distantly muffled through a pillow or grimy garage windows
the car somewhere running
wasting all that energy
stores are closed that I never noticed
their neon signs stay on all day even on Sunday
for no reason today is Sunday

                                        "Is someone in there?"

the general becomes the particular
the abstract the circumstantial

                                        I cannot deny my name
                                        when the fireman asks
                                        "do you live here?"

one is the process and one the scene
one is a birthday which appears in no postcard or landscape
whereas strangers round
        corners

both
        kinesis
                and mimesis
the mind and the eyes
where the firemen can become easily asphyxiated
the walk makes him register his breathing
as it registers the terrain
                                or
                it's good to meet up with Mr. Sandman for
                        a while
                                he's funny
                to hear stalking someone
            disappears in obscure underbrush
                        and reappears with a mustache
                his silliness confounded
                                by his dark touch
                    step up
            and his there-there almanac
                where he insists
                        there is no other mood
                        we are always in our caring position
            in the midst of a world that makes us anxious

                                            unexpectedly
seeing a stranger we wish to recognize
but it's not our step-father   but
                        the blue Horizon might be inside the garage
                        sitting running
                        inertia is potential for work, waiting
the crowd turns another circle, a grandpa looking for a chair, there is
nothing resembling this object he begins looking for "a place to sit,"
quite a different proposition, a curb comes up and his knees hit his chin,
sucks down something from the paper sack, while the manufacture of
this useful bump could not sit in a private house   he is trespassing
its use
                                "did you just get home?"
where there's No totality I can't No
how about purely unifying abstraction, No

67

I lie
in a field of anxiety and sense perceptions

                                                    someone asks me
                armies step in unison
                is there danger in every theory?

where is the walkiness of stories
which is not transcription
the feet do not step directly on the keys
but some flood of words constantly quoting   remembering
the telling tells what happened as it is not as it was
the constant crux of the promise has no direction

my walk had a purpose, I thought
wrong, it's wherever I find myself in it
a silence is not a description, "but there are transitions"

desire which alone is a moment of narrative nothingness
I want to say
                            I was coming home for a ride downtown
        but I step back

                                        angles of the house
                                        meet in the garage
                                        the firemen push the crowd
                                so that the Horizon can't be seen
                                        for curiosity's sake

 walking through your part is different than walking into your part
                            the woman who lives upstairs
comes to the door, panicked and smiling for the flashing red lights
                            she is not who is expected
                            isn't even dressed
the garage becoming crowded   the invisible   the noxious thing
the odorless and impossible   mother?
the neighbor steps down a step too many and stumbles when she
sees me   reaching out for me   saying mother
I was never   her subject
                                                    I was just her occasion
                                                    a sufficient reason

telling anyone, me, that I am grown up, we never are and unlike
nests, which I did collect and know when they are abandoned
there is no such thing as territory without a territorial animal

does an accidental walking, stumbling, tripping, dancelike words awk-
ward, marching? Mosquitoes love us as a warm meal and we view the hills
as soul-enhancers to be mined
to stop
I turn "away" and "turn back" not the clock but the walk over here from
what seems like hours ago now just a few simple images

though as I stand here staring   pile of rocks
I am still stepping   pile of shit
just more slowly   pile of leaves
a story   pile of skins
is only an artifact   pile of napkins
a walk   pile of cigarettes
disappears   pile of papers

what merits celebration   not getting older
where the walking ends   a pile of unretouched photos
or the open field of what is fast becoming a story, impossibly
where is the arrival and departure desk
what is too far to walk   where is impossible to get

the sun squats watching the organization   of onlookers
distinctly nonextinct   all the debris
"there is no such thing as an empty space   the tools and hoses
or an empty time"   outside the garage
                                             intended for the
                                             sidewalk garden
                                             where   now in the
                                             mayhem I can tell
                                             nothing is out of
                                             place except
maddening   the front door wide
                                             open

and fractals of frowning strangers

the infinite complexity of representing a smooth line
in close proximity
a walk
obliterates the math of machinery   promises to collapse

into an example

on the one hand   *birthday* is now unperceived
each object carefully noted   renamed
and reflected
as it balances on the curb of disappearing
into an abstract category as the mind passes by
in the notebook of the body
that there is or isn't a thematic center
the clothing the walker wears
the weight of the knapsack
the weather routine
the purpose of the trip downtown to meet some friends
the numb changing time of day
        leisurely colors
        incremental adjusting textures
        and falling sounds
        a stench a Sunday
        the spacing of things
        the non-declaring of things
        tupperware of feeble samples
        of lunch leftovers
        inconsequential or accidental
        a soda, or
        'had I only gotten here a few minutes earlier . . . '
                the mother still missing
                the nominalist anti-abstractionist she
                for a long time spoke only in specific
                names and named as she
                paced the rooms naming and running
                outside her mind a territory
                each thing a thing with a unique name
                took her to me   finally
                        to a silence

since every word is already an
abstraction or category, especially "me"
specifically leads to nothing
without an inevitable crowd of
bystanders
private rooms are possible only right
before death

a neighborly woman pulls
my sleeve I join to hear the
mumbling as her mind
plays with the world before
her not fixed like the sirens
and the flashing blue red
she walks fast great-aunt
Gertrude I sing blue red the
slippery arhythmia of an old
neighbor with the retarded
country the aria in
recombination tasting of
nonsense or coexistence
of a crowded rubber-
necking consciousness
and a crowd   her
understanding is an ongoing
meditation stepping onto
the elevator of blue-red
reality a way of happening
or "beginning again and
again" she kindly urges me
to move on or to find
another way downtown

there are never completed actions
a sudden opening from underneath, the garage door flips up
with muscle from the firemen
revealing the Horizon in a slanted "on" position running as it were in
place, poison — is it possible— it's true a dog notices the squirrel but
not the sparrow — that in the corner near the leaf-blower the family dog
accidentally succumbed to what is

odorless and invisible

doubt the sight of the door   not to think I might
but turn the knob   have been born
the cold brass is there to be valued   to end up here
rendered to a path
of using everything   of each journey
which has an out-of-place subject
yesterday I found a knife at the park and made it a tool
and the world treated me differently
I cared in a whole new way
could be the same, now that I'm no longer at home at home
as taking the pen or the photograph
too many objects
and a persistent world   an ashtray
in which the story is lodged concretely   a chair
          when the step-father bangs the dinner table   an ashtray
the characters feel   a chair
anchored in an ever-changing point of reference   a recess
he isn't quite real   a bump
sealed in a Horizon we should choose not to open

walking the overgrowth of words flushed to their edges
              of not-stepping not through trees
but to sample the landscape
flushed in speaking it
as it enters   as we look for it
incessantly and instinctually
          becoming   a birthday
a story   so abstract
          a step in the dark   is it a swamp
a bog a wetland sewage plant   the bus schedule's worn off
a dark   "calm down"
homey sensation   I'm stuck walking around
                                        now stuck going nowhere
a family recipe   no really, some shit
that never tastes the same
when someone else makes it

the texture of a walk is vicious, quoted, unseparated, halfway between liq-
uid and solid, hallucinogenic paralysis, a rush that cannot be held in mind,
shaped into direct perceptions giving way to abstraction, a simple line of
infinite points hardened by the fluidity of time, static promise, a dictio-
nary not that words are things but that things are already words, caught in
culture and narratives pre-existing, co-creating the neighborhood, to gos-
sip and shape the history of a family

still I want to
step onto the page
    with variable succession

breaths and silences
dimensions
of thought

    "voice"
    "action"
    "character"
    "setting" "situation"

capturing the flee of experience

how does the purposive nature of
"going someplace" affect the story

the speeding "keep it moving as fast as you can"

drive off the sunset
touch myself

the debris leaves
the deafness of the
elderly or
the watermarks of
drinking glasses
put down so long
even the stain
has aged I didn't
need her anyway
just the way she
could drive, not her
opinions of
what makes the
"good life" and
lose my detached
posture

always can get a ride
one is as good as another
they say
the child's name really
belongs to the parent
"my name" is as nonspecific
as *my name* except when I hear it

a woman screams
to me and my area
is aroused

                    and slowing   as is the space
the direction of necessity, on any level   that my concerns
the fate of the smallest accidental ornamental nothing   inhabit
the creation of a blooming field
of verbal intrusion
                    randomly   "put your smile
of any mathematical or situational variety   back on girl, you've
                                                         got a life
          steps   to lead"
and continuous motion   I'm sorry did I hear
can change a face, a position entirely   you say "wait up"
and finally
one perception must immediately be followed in a direction
and where there has been
no short cut

                                                         the ambulance pulls
no summary   away from the home
                                                         the address marks
                                                         a place where
                                                         something actually
                                                         came to rest not to
                                                         sleep but what is
                                                         called "stopped"

where far as far means
                              the return
          what is always
                         the non-return
                         the spiral
                         parabola
                    "hymn to possibility"
               and other non-returning curves
                         alone
along
                                             a non-returning path
of I'll take the bus downtown instead
                                                  anything
that attempts a walk
                    encourages the principle of Forgetting

in Reading

                                                        or Walking

every forgetting

                                                    is no allegory

is a remembering

                                        is an assertion of freedom

from which the mind steps from

                                                        a different

step

                                        another journey

or approaching

                            a stopping place

                pause

to see the doorway

            examine the keyhole for a sign of strangers

smell the different recipe
of time and cement
or the recent rain
names of different soups in similar cans
and look toward what has already happened
and look back at the page
or across the misting street

where

                                        they say no one sees anything
                                                    coming

                out again

a different hour

                        another route

            would not say

what
           this one

                              did

HOURS

Empty Set 1: [Islands]

In most *ex nihilo* creation myths the single god-figure creates the world by Thinking, Speaking or Breathing; i.e., *"Nobody could have mistaken them unless he had windmills in his brain"* (Sancho Panza). The windmills have created his very brain.

ACT 1: /THE WORD OF THE LIGHT/

A monkey and organ-grinder play upon hearts, for memory-money, lustfully with their master-and-puppet or pet routine, a ploy for other people's passion, small geysers or pennies, dimes or recognitions, quarters or prayers, epiphanies of powerlessness, lower orders, gargoyles. Rock stars appear around the eyes of passers-by, spouting coins. The organ-grinder considers at least one ego-driven creation which can't be undone by slight-of-hand behind the ear or out the sleeve but can be made safe by staying two nights in [the best tourist trap in the world] and seducing the monkey with [3 emotional treats].

Monkey.	It seems we'll never make a penny off it.
Organ Grinder.	Nope, never a single encounter. [what it means to earn a "living"]
Monkey.	[7 outdated objects which dangle]
Organ Grinder.	Not even one beautiful bonnet, with ribbons.
Monkey.	if only — [a famous opera phrase]
Organ Grinder.	[the first uses of photography]
Monkey.	[the process of gathering forensic evidence]
Organ Grinder.	if only — [an adhoc hobo song]
Monkey.	[3 things that can easily be faked]

The species divides, one great part going That Way, the other surrendering to a desk; she has an urge to do something perverse upon her world, becoming a strange and drunken genie playing ukulele, saying "hello" forever; a temporary spell.

ACT 2: /THE REFLECTION IN THE WATER/

When she came home from the party she burned for three months, exhaling newly formed molecules without refueling. Through her shadow she saw [2 signs that the universe is in motion] and thought: *it is three a.m. in the east.* It is earlier in the west, though they ended sooner. She stumbles straight into her unformatted child; a bicycle falls down the front stairs and is grievously injured. She loved the organ-grinder but loathed the act — there is no one to take care of her in her hour of desire.

Bicycle.	[how it feels to have an idea]
Unformatted Child.	Some people are simply allergic, it means nothing to them.
Bicycle.	I've loved you since [the process of a soul's transmigration]
Unformatted Child.	[3 symptoms of epilepsy]
Bicycle.	(*stuttering*) [3 signs of God in the Flesh]
Unformatted Child.	[the process of delusion]
Bicycle.	Why did you say you weren't happy here anyway?
Unformatted Child.	[how to talk yourself into a corner]
Bicycle.	[why air becomes turbulent]

Just then the avenues converge and the stairway sinks into a strike of oil. Large dogs lumber over and lap until they are fattened and slow. Black umbrellas open across the eastern sky. She tries to remember exactly what was said during the trick. [3 hometown newspapers] flutter westward with unbearable certainty, emptying facts in uncharted lakes. She thinks that perhaps she will build up anti-bodies and return to the midway.

ACT 3: /THE MESSENGER ACTIVATES THE LONGING/

Her legs are unshaven, veins bulging close to the skin, bruised with chocolate. Chocolate sings folk songs and she languishes. This could have been her sexiest hour. The sleep appears in the afternoon, and just when she feels like mentioning it to someone, it sits on her tongue. The television beckons with "[5 revelations]." [Why movies resemble suicide when watched on video]. There isn't anything she can do to stop the unwatered plants. [Why suicides never videotape themselves].

Plants.	Whatever.
Sleep.	[A blanket of historical data]
Plants.	Sure.
Sleep.	[A sheet of facts and information]
Plants.	Whatever.
Sleep.	[A pillow of theoretical jargon]
Plants.	Could you find me a drink?
Sleep.	[3 ways to know if you have neurological damage]
Plants.	Nevermind.

For the first three winters she thought napping was a faze, something in her immune system, something relating to her inner growth of sugar. She vowed to sleepwalk to the next town. Only after the third unformatted child turned up dead did she realize the house was convulsive. Diverting her brain waves from mirrors and other undomesticated surfaces, focusing them instead on the body temperature of earthworms and the opening of take-out menus, she vowed to move to Alaska. She was contaminated with an epilepsy of snacking. The house a compost heap of unfinished thoughts.

ACT 4: /ANCIENT CIVILIZATION/

Haves and have-nots walk a tree-lined street. A truck bears down, knocking over the biggest tree, injuring those who had not loved it. Screams can be counted inside the city. Haves run one way, joining their laughter together. A shapely woman arrives in a warping ambulance. A mechanic leans out the window and witnesses as the tree dies in her arms and an unexplained drop in third-grade reading scores brings down the economy of the entire region. A scar appears in the flesh of the sidewalk and never quite heals.

Haves.	Deaf children on the subways read minds.
Have-nots.	[the personal implication of "data-base"]
Haves.	It's always raining when you leave the dermatologist.
Have-nots.	[the cultural implication of "stereographic" projection]
Haves.	People often think their lover would make a great president.
Have-nots.	[the political implication of unrequited love]
Haves.	History repeats itself every time you think about it.
Have-nots.	[the economic implication of shutting the fuck up]
Haves.	A slap in the face.

The street has a large cut down her cheek, and hides by turning the other one. Negligent people walk there. Dogs lift their legs and trickle into her squinty eye. She blinks back the exhaust. Rakes scrape her forehead as she takes leaves from her senses.

ACT 5: /HOW THE DOG GOT ITS FUR/

The figure hangs out with the ground in a summer rest-area near Duluth. A glowing tour-bus empties people with cameras flashing. In front of the information tableau the figure makes mental notes in the dust of a back windshield. Ground argues the other side and they enjoy the sudden distance between them (knowing they will soon be back in the gasoline odor of summer forgiveness). Ground pulls his skin into the figure of a colorful butterfly reformatting into grass.

Figure.   [How to recognize a "throe" of passion]
Ground.   [The best way to look for a job]
Figure.   [3 symptoms of false perspective]
Ground.   Can't you even describe a double point?
Figure.   [7 ways love is neurological]
Ground.   [a really good how-the-dog-got-its-fur story]
Figure.   Ironically, the accuracy suffers at the node.
Ground.   [the process of hoping for something]
Figure.   But the country will take care of us, right?

The coke machine is mercilessly raped. Maps get some genuine affection and the brochures dive jealously beneath the plastic tables. [2 great thinkers of the age] hang out near the phone booths, accepting calls. As the highway bill passes the senate, caterpillars fear to begin. Figures in the woods start gaining ground and vocabulary. Grounds for divorce become exponentially impossible.

ACT 6: /THE CREATIVE GERM/

A runway cuts through the island at dusk; a locus of bacteria in lights. From the airplane she was able to spot an hour's worth of earth that seemed free from disease. But as they approached the village, there was evidence of focal regression in the cells along the coast. Apparently, the margins were not clean and no further incision had been made. The lights were active and unusual. This would allow the asymmetrical industrial communities to spread throughout the forest, even up onto the glaciers.

Glacier.	[5 signs of vanity]—[3 ways to undo a commitment]
Bacteria.	Hey Pal. We need a little more room to spread out.
Glacier.	[5 signs of insanity]
Bacteria.	You scratch our back.
Glacier.	[how long being "in love" lasts]
Bacteria.	We're already plural.
Glacier.	[8 modest protestations]
Bacteria.	Don't take that tone with us, Frosty.
Glacier.	[5 signs of urbanity]

Planes land; the virus is airborne. The center for disease-control polls 10,000 people who have recently moved to states they perceive as full of "undeveloped wilderness" and determine that most of them say they are moving for the love of something. As the plane makes its final approach, the disease has spread into all the remaining tissues of darkness.

ACT 7: /THE NOISY CHANNEL/

A storm, by cleaning the data in the distance, blips on screen; he sighs as the symbols turn upside down and emotions rust a gate function open. The mine through the mountain went bust in the thawing, but not the algorithms, still sharp when you step on them. Boys invite girls to play in the razor-wire that surrounds the prison. "Someday we will live there, just you and me," they promise on channels branching with noise and nothing to smooth them. Without the aid of strong mental banks, the radars cannot find comfortable positions in the language.

Zeros.	Why did you want to marry me?
Ones.	[3 features of a silent movie]
Zeros.	Nothing for verbal or harmonic reasons?
Ones.	[3 features of a ballet]
Zeros.	What if the impulse pattern were reversed?
Ones.	[detailed description of the best place you ever made love]
Zeros.	{what it's like to be a moment of peace}
Ones.	[the least romantic experience of your life]
Zeros.	[the process of changing from a liquid to a solid]

When the final example doesn't happen, the weather service pretends there have never been consecutive days. They didn't mean the storm was on its <u>way</u>, not way, but someday, there'd be a storm <u>someday</u>. Dumbshits. Grammar dead-ends into the blue screen of untrackable eyes.

ACT 8: /A TURTLE ENDS UP IN ALASKA/

The pilots train differently when the fairy tales split at take-off. Daredevils auto-pilot the calendars and accelerate opinions, testing for wind-shear and moss. In the mile-wide television studio, knights await news of life. When a birth draws near, the dragons put up heat-deflecting radar defense shields. Fathers turn quickly into loggers or stew-tasters, stone lay-ers, captains, and embers. The rock stars wonder what roles they may fall into if they set out past dark without matches. This is not a good time to be hun-gry. The little pathfinder sits on its distant planet and wonders if anyone still listens to its thoughts.

Martians.	I'll trade you my life for half a dozen eggs.
Photos.	[2 favorite smells]
Martians.	Did you bring a dictionary so I can make repairs?
Photos.	[2 bad thoughts]
Martians.	Eggs make the best sleeping bags.
Photos.	[5 invisible things]
Martians.	I want to fix the little Rover with tree sap and alas there are no trees.
Photos.	[3 reasons why we can't commit to the idea of life on Mars]
Martians.	[4 reasons why we can commit to the idea of life on Mars]

It doesn't matter that the windows are filthy in space.
It doesn't matter what your hair looks like in space.
It doesn't matter if you're an hour late in space.
It doesn't matter if you have performance anxiety in space.
It doesn't matter if you have baggage from a previous relationship
    in space.
It doesn't matter if there is God or Allah or [children's cartoon characters]
    in space.

An army going up the escalator gets trapped between floors. The cafeteria hovers blissfully. Two people in love claim all the jello for their benefit. A very tall person appears. The organ-grinder feeds his pet in a separate booth. There is a breach of security when the bananas open — the smell so thick the soldiers roll their lips back and put their nostrils in their pockets. Chrome reflects in their eyes. People in love don't eat full meals. The chemical warfare is not announced.

Very Tall Person.	I've never been able to eat bananas plain like that.
Escalator.	{3 positive aspects of extinction}
Very Tall Person.	Sometimes on cereal, or with yoghurt, but never just plain like that.
Escalator.	{the reason why practice makes perfect}
Very Tall Person.	I've just never liked them. Not plain like that; it's just something funny about how I've always been.
Escalator.	{why you sometimes feel off-balance}
Very Tall Person.	I don't know why.
Escalator.	{17 ways not to tell someone you love them}
Very Tall Person.	{definition, "relative"}

He enters a long lunch-line cafeteria, with homicidal rice pudding. An old flame is there, warming scrambled eggs, hoping to serve some up to him. There is the pudding again with proof floating in it. The armies are in the freezer section. She can't bring a fork to her lips while her bicycles are still melting. A heat lamp shines directly on a roast beef, free-standing among parsley. The escalators jerk forward and the nightly news resumes. He doesn't feel like paying for his meal. The hotel will bill his room. The key to hosting the summit is how the bedrooms are arranged. Nightly ministers take care of the business the handshakes conceal.

Act 10: /the AND-Gate Signals/

All the screens are blank, except one which is broken. One lover conceals a weapon and the other quickly tries to order one. She had really hoped the shoot-out would keep its sleeves disheartened but the brawl was mentioned early in the film and needed erupting. If she looks at her opponent she will throw him a kiss. She must keep her eyes insular but the broken screens cause the couple to reroute into the corral. The monkey costume is exhausted from over-use. Still, until someone fires first, it remains unclear whether the meeting is friendly. Some horses ask to be stolen and elope with bullets flying.

Concealed.	[what the ancient warriors saw]
Weapon.	[what the sun said when she looked at the earth]
Concealed.	[the ways pre-nuptial agreements can help]
Weapon.	[the reasons why kissing evolved as it did]

A shot is fired into the air

Concealed.	[the reason for non-aggression among the Bonobo chimps]
Weapon.	[how to change your mind about someone]
Concealed.	[the process of getting a sunburn]
Weapon.	[what good it does to show your emotions]
Concealed.	[what good lawyers do for their clients]

Quietly, without waking anyone, the Moon People gather around their snakes. No matter how hard they whisper, they cannot get their shadows to back them up. The police arrive and divide the married from the unmarried sheriffs. There is a moment when everyone thinks the gunman might ejaculate spastically. But then the sugar kicks back in and the symptom of false sentiment, [a contemporary love song], soothes the dusty town. While he is sleeping so soundly near the campfire, she considers buck-knifing his throat. But alas, no Martians.

ACT 11: /NOW EACH OF THE TURTLES HAS A RING/

She returns home after spending her first night in a "strange" bed. The floor won't look up to her and the locks have rotted. She moves toward infinity then back on the smallest changes in vowels. She brushes the hair back from her unscannable child, who kicks her in the shin and speaks Chinese. In school they teach all the children Chinese, and some parents are getting worried. She would like to make herself a sandwich. She would like to commit to a video. Perhaps she would even like to walk out the window. A path finds her mercilessly excepted.

Strange Bed.	I'm glad it happened.
Home.	[definition, "abstract"]
Strange Bed.	I'm just sitting here with no opinions.

Home.	[definition, "askance"]
Strange Bed.	I am a strange and uncommon attractor.
Home.	[definition, "artful"]
Strange Bed.	Is there anything I can say to make you feel better?
Home.	[definition, "Alchemical Creation"]
Strange Bed.	[how to captivate an audience]

An asymptote propels itself between channels: the telephone rings. The lover's approach is curved, but still cannot convince her to put down the knife and spare the rib. She will not answer. What the postman does on Monday is of no consequence now. She once forgave membership in the society of go-getters and set the remote within reach. Whatever happened, she thinks, was only the beginning, and I can still ignore it. Of course the particular images weigh heavily in her glands and she spends the afternoon remixing the house.

ACT 12: /EX NIHILO/

The lovers' faces appear on many of the screens. It is the 16th century; it is Mauritius. It is a strip mall. It is 1462. It is a "neighborhood." It is a national park. It is an apartment. It is a town. It is an anthill. It is an idea. It is a phone number. It's in the cards. It's on the tips of their tongues. It is a path of sun across a lake. It is a tiny clone of eternity.

First Lover.	[why no person is an island]
Second Lover.	[3 favorite qualities of First Lover speaking]
First Lover.	[3 favorite qualities of Second Lover speaking]
Second Lover.	[the reasons for high rates of extinction on islands]
First Lover.	[the reasons that the most extravagant and unusual species evolve on islands]
Second Lover.	[how you feel about First Lover right now, and why]
First Lover.	[3 differences between chance and fate]
Second Lover.	[23 endangered or extinct species]
First Lover.	[how you feel about Second Lover right now, and why]

The void is the blank of the screen of the nothing, the empty set of minds, grotesque witnesses just before the wind, a brief rain or insufficient dictionary, gives format to the future. The lovers take a long unreadable look at the gates between them. The crashed child takes off on her bicycle before you can stop her. She may not be back for dinner, or for bedtime, or for breakfast, or for anything you had planned. The circuits dip into surging, anticipating the family.

EMPTY SET 2: [FAMILY]

Sets of four are equally alive as sets of two, and equally empty. [Family] contains [Islands] but elaborates the evolutionary paths found between diverse yet proximal species. Magical neotenous evolutions are likely but unprovable, taking their places within different gates of the amplified set: [why we give birth to our own kind] and including [the laws governing the time required for wounds to heal: biological time] and [4 life-support environments]. *"Camouflaged in crackling seas, the Continuous Creationists remain unanswered by hydrogen or heaven"; the atoms form galaxies just like ours, but when gravitation fails them they fall apart. The universe breathes again and the action movie gets set to reruns, thus stirring the dangerous beginnings of "family life."*

ACT 13: NIPPERS OF NINEVEH

In the submarine, the pressure of the water varies and the light through the water refracts differently just like she said it would. They have become members of a set of coincidences. A rope falls silently at the base of their stomachs, forcing air to escape where it can. The others connect to the same oxygen source, exchanging verticality for the long-run. A herd collects and plunges through the leagues; their costumes bind them safely.

Time is Money.	[def., "convenience"]
Time is Personal.	Oh, brother. Wet costumes stink.
Time is Money.	[how you know Time is Personal]
Time is Personal.	[the story of *Robinson Crusoe*] You can't come in a room when the door's shut.
Time is Money.	[4 considerations in designing a boat]
Allowance.	I'm thinking. [2 reasons why "doorbells"]
Discipline.	[4 things children never appreciate about their parents]
Allowance.	[stages of boredom]
Discipline.	[steps to making a calendar]
Time is Money.	I'm late for practice. [why "business suits"]
Allowance.	[the parts of a submarine][how a water molecule sticks together] [2 reasons you can't unmake dinner once it's made]
Time is Personal.	[4 visions of the future] [how you know Time is Money] I didn't choose this.

Discipline.	[definition, "information"]
Allowance.	You're one to talk. [1 story about Time is Money] Someone else made me say this.
Discipline.	[how you know these people]
Time is Personal.	[definition, "chance"]
Time is Money.	[calculation of the cost of taking a NYC taxi to the bottom of the Atlantic Ocean]
Allowance.	[description of "specious time"]
Time is Personal.	The information rush of data through our nervous systems, or else [3 sentence retelling of a famous family drama]
Discipline.	[why a penny saved is a penny earned]
Time is Money.	[why you're here]
Time is Personal.	[a few things you know about Discipline]
Allowance.	[4 things that never stay clean]
Discipline.	[the properties of Newtonian time]
Time is Money & Time is Personal	[4 ways to tell if parents are divorcing]
Allowance.	[10 types of smiles]
Discipline.	[10 tones of voice]
Time is Money & Time is Personal	[the stages of returning home] [4 things you notice when you meet someone's family]
Discipline.	[the difference between heat and temperature] [2 things you know about Allowance]
Allowance.	[4 ways to split atoms equally]
Discipline.	[enactment of the first time you had to take care of a parent]
Allowance.	[enactment of the first time you realized a parent couldn't take care of you]
Time is Money.	[4 things it's better not to know]
Time is Personal.	[4 ways to get out of doing something]
Discipline.	[2 common parental threats]
Allowance.	[describe the faces of others]
Discipline.	[what you're doing here]
Time is Money.	Just try to forget I said anything.
Time is Personal.	[2 reasons to throw money at something]
Long Pause.	

Allowance.	[16 sea creatures]
Discipline.	[how it feels to have no sense where life is heading]
Allowance.	Shhhh.
Discipline.	[8 things you can't hear]
Time is Personal.	[the best way to make someone feel better]
Time is Money.	[how you know you're related to someone]
Time is Personal.	[4 ways to escape from a submarine]

ACTS 14-22: STABLEMATES

A great crescendo rips through the family. Whole herds of mammals plunge off cliffs. Other flocks rise into Olympic villages. Burglar alarms are lullaby babies. Celebrate the moments of your answering machine. Fireplaces as large as lakes incinerate the hallucinations of a generation of rock-stars.

Rock Star.	[4 excellent aspects of being a rock star]
Bandmate.	[2 ways to tell if you've gotten a girl pregnant]
Roadie.	[4 reasons it's hard to be on the road all year]
Fuck Buddy.	[2 tips to keeping your sanity while dating a married man]

The amphitheater fills with rats, each licking itself clean. Each seat near the stage is a grave until risen from. Nobody belongs in English. Dancing is the ecstatic expression of a curfew and homework, but mystical advantage goes to those children whose virginity has never been dismantled.

President.	[4 things that have always been illegal]
Chairman.	[2 things that were illegal and now aren't]
Lobbyist.	[2 reasons sports, rock, and movie stars out-earn everyone else]
Voter.	[4 ways you can tell if someone has memorized what they're saying]

A doorbell, followed by complete inflation. After a moment, the system reboots. A suburban dwelling with all the trimmings. There isn't anything to drink.

Pride.	I agree.
Prejudice.	I agree.
Old.	Yup.
Same Old.	You bet.

Dinner creeps from the information closet.

North.   [describe the science of "reverse speech"]
East.   [2 things you learned by watching television]
West.   [the 4 best things about your parents]
South.   [4 features of being in a cult]

White noise. White out. Pure as the. Absorbs all the. Hides. Coats. Soothes. Relieves. A getaway car. Get out of jail free. Own recognizance. Nepotism. Chip off the old block. Why don't you come with me to take a look around the factory, son? There's no need to call the police.

Small.   No.
Medium.   Shh.
Large.   What?
X-tra Large.   [How you know you have fleas]
                              [the steps to getting rid of fleas]
                              [2 ways to ruin someone's career]

The University embarrasses itself. There is a contest in Heaven and the University wins. It is thrown off the mountain and turns into a row of oysters (oysters standing for promiscuity). Crocheted tea-cozies drop from the ceiling, insulating everyone.

Particle.   [4 signs of moral impoverishment]
Embryo.   [silence]
Skeleton.   [silence]
Ijiwrje.   [4 signs that the universe exists in everything]

Laughter from the cans of paint. One by one the brushes lift themselves out of the sink and migrate toward the windows, smacking genealogies on the glass. The job of disinfection is only half-finished and the guests are here.

China.   [1 reason a child might feel older than her grandparent]
India.   [enactment of reading a top-notch thriller]
Russia.   [enactment of watching a realistic family drama]
Antarctica.   [1 reason it's weird when two people look in the same
                mirror at the same time]

An argument breaks out. Everyone clutches their corn. Some run toward forgiveness but the elders have it cornered. They shoot to kill. The weekend is overthrown.

Boss.   [4 effects of watches on love]

Underling.   [4 effects of watches on business]

Middle-Manager.   [4 effects of watches on food]

Worker.   [2 effects of watches on armies]

All four family members enter the vehicle from the back. Driving across self-sterilized open spaces, their volume is turned way up as they each tackle new time-zones. The mother finally confronts her desk as the father and son make meaningful canoeing.

Money.   [the time sense of parents in relation to subways]

Wilderness.   [the time sense of children in relation to bees]

Beauty.   [the time sense of lovers in relation to computers]

Death.   [the time sense of anti-matter in relation to everything else]

The Idea of Family crosses upstage. All train their eyes. All eyes adjust to the dark. All Ideas are final. There isn't any indication if it's a good idea or a bad idea. The Idea passes without speaking.

Neighbor.   [features of Hopi societal structure]

Neighbor.   [a Hopi story]

Neighbor.   [the verb tenses of the Hopi]

Neighbor.   [contemporary politics of the Hopi]

With that, the child announces her plans to turn the family house into an orchid ranch. The parents are encouraged to travel to the thirteenth century. Once in suspended animation, the children stop whispering. Best intentions wrapped in newspapers grow fungus on the back porch and time passes this little cast of characters by.

Set Designer.   [design the perfect family home]

Director.   [cast the perfect types in each role]

Costume Designer.   [pick the perfect fabrics and accessories]

Actor.   [4 lame acceptance speeches]

                            [1 nasty off-the-cuff remark]

Reality sets in. This time, no one is jumping for the phone. Relatives kept at too great a distance tend not to give presents. The medication blunts their libraries. {3 common lies about the importance of family} splash across the animated faces of irony.

Swamp.	[exhale on a pitch and hold it]
Spider.	[inhale on a pitch and hold it]
Microbes.	[vibrate on a pitch and hold it]
Whales.	[2 verses from a favorite song]

And from here, to eternity. That's all folks. The gig is up. The family is finally resting peacefully, after such a difficult struggle. If it grows back, call your doctor. If it spreads to your whole community, take comfort in the certain autointoxication of meaning that will result.

ACT 23: OYSTER BEDS IN THE OZONOSPHERE

Airborne now, the family is shuttling, weightless. The articles pass among subjects. The paragraphs end before sentences. There is nothing holding the reader's attention except some marginalia. Good conjunctions are nowhere to be found and the syntax is atrocious. The zoo has not been copyrighted and the beasts are evolving toward deep space when fed into the computer.

Father.	[how to write a good topic sentence]
Child.	[def., "subordinate clause"]
Mother.	I'm being forced to say this.
Father.	Someone is putting words in my mouth.
Child.	[def., "paranoia"]
Child.	[def., "panorama"]
Mother.	Wait a minute, I'd never say any of these words in a million years; they're so cliché.
Father.	What's happening to us?
Mother.	[4 things parents threaten their children with] I didn't want to say this.
Father.	[2 punishments]
Child.	[1 thing a director says to actors]
Child.	[def., "freedom"]
Father.	I didn't want to say this; I'm just repeating what other fathers said.

Child.	[describe the process of learning your lines]
Mother.	[def., "corollary"]
Father.	[describe the "time of things"]
Mother.	I don't seem to be able to change this.
Child.	[4 similes for Mother starting with, "Mom's like a . . . "]
Father.	[4 similes starting with, "You're like a . . . "]
Child.	[12 meanings of "Mute"]
Child.	[what happens if actors mutiny]
Father.	[what you love about your family]
Mother.	[what you love about what you're doing right now]
Children.	[2 alternatives to eating or drinking from cows]
Child.	[why your family is typical]
Child.	[why you love your parents]

EMPTY SET 3: [THE PICTURE OF DORIAN GRAY]

The inevitable (re)surfacing of the individual – represented by the number "6" – the ideal of perfection – the shadow that pursues love, the shadow forgetting its origin. Language-piano is the condition and critique of virtuosity — aria, monologue — standing in for duration, the role of experience, the condition of art, and probably delusion. The same impossibility of stasis or terminal equilibrium exists between the relationships in this set (1:1) as in the others. *From the soup, a single individual is made, a billion of them. What is impractical are the things we cherish: dreams in which we make the world according to any sort of logic. "If a person can't be certain which light will light when he presses a button, then the viewer can't be certain which button was pressed when a certain light lights." The invisible billion finds expression in the single example.*

ACT 24: 88 KEYS TO THE INDIVIDUAL

THERE	[6 examples of negative feedback]
WAS	[your first heartbreak]
SOMETHING	[3 ways to make something stick to the wall]
TERRIBLY	[2 favorite foods]
ENTHRALLING	[the functions of versification]
IN	[why some cities have "Mischief Night" in addition to Halloween]
THE	[def., "narcissism"]
EXERCISE	[mathematical definition of "branch"]
OF	[steps to making a sound]
INFLUENCE	[6 uses of masks]
NO	[why someone would enter the priesthood or a convent]

OTHER	[the history of the "anti-masque"]
ACTIVITY	[3 "ugly" colors]
LIKE	[an elegy to someone you loved]
IT	[the difference between empathy and sympathy]
TO	[why the frogs are disappearing from the earth]
PROJECT	[def., "suspension of disbelief"]
ONE'S	[how to fake cry]
SOUL	[3 examples of Carpe Diem]
INTO	[an aube]
SOME	[explanation of "a knock is as good as a boost"]
GRACIOUS	[2 children's rhymes]
FORM	[def., "action at a distance"]
AND	[the 6 best features of your hometown]
LET	[2 reasons to be celibate]
LIFE	[3 ways that food hunts you]
TARRY	[2 features of a talk show]
THERE	[why a promise is like a hairdryer]
FOR	[6 things people do to stay attractive]
A	[2 reasons you think you are unique]
MOMENT	[why "when the frog flies into his passion, the pond knows nothing of his tantrum"]
HEAR	[2 reasons not to look in a mirror when you're depressed]
OWN	[3 peace-time uses of submarines]
INTELLECTUAL	[def., "laissez-faire"]
VIEWS	[how to explain an alphabet to someone who can't read]
ECHOED	[3 good reasons to learn another language]
BACK	[the number of relatives you see every year]
ONE	[sample of iambic pentameter]
WITH	[two lines from your favorite song]
ALL	[6 words in Chinese]
ADDED	[2 things you'd change about your life]
MUSIC	[how to lie with the devil]
PASSION	[def., "superstition"]
YOUTH	[a story of unrequited love]
CONVEY	[3 lessons your father taught you about life]
TEMPERAMENT	[the first time you did something illegal]
ANOTHER	[everything you've ever won]

AS	[def., "experiment"]
THOUGH	[2 examples of something "poetic"]
WERE	[2 experiences of the supernatural]
SUBTLE	[a quote from your favorite writer]
FLUID	[3 things your mother taught you about love]
OR	[3 words in the language of the Hopi]
STRANGE	[description of the kinds of things you think about while masturbating]
PERFUME	[the most aggravating commercial jingle]
NEVER	[the worst thing you ever saw done to an animal]
REAL	[3 examples of "Problem" plays]
JOY	[6 things to do if you don't understand something]
THAT	[2 signs of winter]
EVERY	[most of any popular song]
PORTRAIT	[what you would say if suddenly everyone in the world were listening to you]
PAINTED	[6 electronic "spaces" and do they really exist]
FEELING	[6 reasons you watch television]
ARTIST	[6 good things about bacteria]
NOT	[why a coffin is like a streetlight]
SITTER	[the history of "closet" dramas]
REVEAL	[3 kinds of stress]
ART	[how a computer is like a honeymoon]
CONCEAL	[2 differences between closets and hallways]
SEX	[a scientific experiment which tests whether love is stronger than hate]
ART'S	[how a subway is like an urge]
AIM	[def., "weak ending"]
DISCORD	[3 outdated slang words]
TO BE	[a song with special romantic significance]
FORCED	[why people do things they don't like to do]
HARMONY	[the closest you ever came to rape]
OTHERS	[6 really beautiful people of your sex]
FIRST	[2 things you'd change about your family]
GREATEST	[3 definitions of "mandate"]
BUT	[3 meaningless phrases]
PREPARATION	[2 things you'd change about your looks]
IF	[3 things that embarrass you]

DOESN'T   [6 things you hate in theater]
TALK   [why traditions should be honored]
ABOUT   [6 words in a language you don't speak]
THING   [the thing you love most about yourself]
HAPPENED   [3 things you'd change about tonight]
LOVE   [def., "love"]

SEVEN VEILS

Comets

Bodies vary in importance and distance from the star. Bodies can be sand-sized or huge.
Sal was seen by early people dancing on her hands, her feet dangling by her ears.
She was painted this way with blazing eyes and glowing skin and many saw her.
The sun of the world she knows is only an average one. The moon a low-grade rock.
But they center the system and so are important and familiar and exert this power.
On an average day, people may not know exactly where Sal is and they may wonder.
She spends her time as someone's sentence: looking like, at, how.

Other bodies include satellites and moons, soldiers, step-fathers, prophets.
Sal wanders farthest past the sun at the edge of this limited imagination.
She walks the beach of the horizon so closely she does not appear to move.
Mike and Sal and Stacey have been friends since the shaded library.
Mike and Stacey know Sal better than anyone and can tell a mood from skin trouble.
Her ears are small, barely noticeable, unless she dangles her ankles around them.
Squint as she passes upside-down and she'll appear to smile.

People interviewed later stress that Sal is not nearly as distant as she was made to look.
Even in broad daylight her total weight is less than most meteors.

They say that Sal is the "nearest approach to nothing that can still be anything."

You are looking at layers of ice, some small particles, some gas.

The hard part of Sal is tiny, but the coma surrounding it can be wider than earth's orbit.

Her coma consists of ammonia, frozen water, iron, and nickel and sweeps the universe clean.

Unlike most, her tail is gentle, a curtain of cotton amnesia.

Left to her own devices, Sal would not shine in the night at all.

When she rounds the sun she is illuminated only by reflection.

There is nothing to her fluorescence but one energy oscillating into another.

Close to the shrill heat of her mother, there's corrosion of her flimsy materials.

Solar wind, pressure from radiation, all of these contribute to her steady wasting.

Every weekend practically there is something to celebrate, some boredom to dispel.

In this frenzy, Stacey helps choose a dress.

Mike teases Sal about her hair and her shadowy shoulders.

He calls her his "dirty little iceball" and she smiles that he loves her enough to name her.

Sal and Mike and Stacey share a secret oath: no superfluous circus.

It was believed by the Greeks that hot evaporations caused Sal's baleful loitering.

Or hot exhalations bursting into flame over kings who insisted the omens were not theirs.

Their enemies, they announced, had better take heed of the hairy torches.

Vespasian, Macrinus, and other emperors perished in the years of their comets nonetheless.

Even with her friends beside her, Sal is mistaken for a corrupter of stars.

She has been accused of earthquakes, famines, and distrust among men.
She has been accused of aiming at earth with suicidal ambition.
End-of-the-world scares occur in all countries.
Herod procures a few hours of blasphemy for a political fundraiser.
Sal can be mistaken for a weapon or an omen as she lingers by the hot tub.
Reason just cannot compete with the misguided faith of insecure men.

During her lifetime, Sal weaves an eccentric circle.
Most bright naked-eye comets can't be forced to the table.
No one was sure how she could be so non-parabolic.
Yet anyone with a certain demeanor twists her orbit violently.
One of these bodies could hurl Sal into deep space altogether.
For this reason, Mike gave Sal his house key and an invitation to crash there anytime.
Amateur comet hunters seek their trophies ruthlessly.

Turns out that the planets in our solar system form an almost perfect plane.
Drawing quietly on sheets of paper, circles within circles, children get it right.
But Sal comes in from other directions, ripping the paper to pieces.
So teachers, parents, governments, downplay her role in the grand design.
Around the children her visit is filtered with idiomatic language.
In most cases a comet is named for its discoverer and labeled with years and letters.
Mike and Stacey know her better than anyone and can't quite find the words either.

Once Sal has been hypothesized, her angle must be found with respect to heaven.
By observing resultant actions she can be tracked by trained eyes.
Displacing the banquet hall, the library, she cuts a swath through each room.
Her face and body tangle dirty looks and muffled laughs into data arrows.
Anyone caught looking directly at her may experience nausea.
She'd displace the most massive mythology for the sake of a peaceful moment.
If only some joker hadn't painted her upside-down with ankles dangling...

Some historical, many mythological, and most celestial beings have long worded lives.
Only Sal and her adolescent friends slip past silently.
Daylight, boredom, curiosity, clouds, overcome them.
Sometimes they pass exceptionally close and once in a thousand years you feel them.
Mike and Stacey tolerate the occasional shattering of Sal into pieces.
In unlit corners of the palace they wait while she reassembles.
Never assume a comet dies; she's often safe in her bedroom by morning.

Whenever Sal breaks apart for good there will be showers of meteorites.
An investigation into Siberia might find a twenty-mile circle of dead reindeer and pine.
But nothing solid, no evidence from the closet or the bank vault.
A visiting ship, a missile, would have left traces of some material.
Most likely the ice in her head simply melts on impact.
Most likely something dirty and delicate evaporates into the atmosphere.
News reporters won't find Mike and Stacey for comment.

It is said that Sal was born from a hot planet, a miniature sun ejecting a chip of itself.

Or perhaps a sun passed through a gravitational cloud which pulled Sal out like a splinter.

Perhaps all the most insubstantial material in the universe pulled together.

Then there are those who think Sal is just the leftovers of all the leftovers.

This would explain why someone's always looking at her, spotting her likeness.

This would explain why she is never liked, never likes to be so looked on, looking like.

Naked-eyed and ankles to ears, she casts curses on amateur astronomers.

Species

The discus fish sucks instinctively but other fish must be taught to take the nipple.

A mother lioness teaches what food to eat and how and where to find it.

Even birds who fly intuitively need demonstrations on the finer points.

The secrets of the air can be taught by either parent or by a "helper" at the nest.

Baby birds of monogamous species develop an ear only for certain pitches.

And they can produce only the exact sequence of notes as the adults who raise them.

Sal called her friends from the gate house and offered them half the kingdom. Plus dinner.

Bring something to watch on television, she adds. Like a cheetah cub she knows she will be left.

The mother cheetah rushes the lessons to get in all the information.

The mother brings prey, half-dead, back to the lair. Go to it, she orders.

The cub isn't strong enough and botches the job while the mother stands by, distracted.

Ready or not, she's gone as fast as any question answered.

Judging by what's written, the human mind is full of rats.
Status on the *scala natura* is based on what you will do at key points in a maze.
Or how quickly you'll humiliate yourself for dinner.
But rats manipulate a complex world beyond the palace walls.
And mice and viruses and ants notice that people aren't learning anything.
Except how best to test how well they can test what little they know how to test for.

A kangaroo is unaware of giving birth and so escapes knowing of her cruelties.
She is able to neglect, without stress or guilt, a less than perfect baby.
If the tiny newborn falls to the ground, the mother will not reach down and help her.
Her nipple is waiting but if the girl becomes detached, then *de facto* she's unfit.
A hardy infant will cling so tightly she can't be dislodged for all the tea in china.
But faced with danger the mother clears her pouch of any child found there.

The king once thought if you kill half the frog in the egg, you end up with half a frog.
No one who sees Sal can predict how she'll look in other circumstances.
Baboon daughters study protocol from their mothers: which favors for which leaders.
Is she maze dull, bright? Genetically, is she less than likely to survive?
She displays discontinuous stereotypes.
Glancing at her mother's cleavage, that first selfish gene, Sal sees an enormous shadow.

The king is a scientist of behavior and restricts evolution to his one priceless prisoner.
Populations tend to overproduce the pretty, while the altruistic and zealous die.

Eventually everyone resembles the survivors; everyone comes from a real winner.
Basic bio as the king understands it.
Only the urine, raised lips, bristled back, indicate to Sal what he's on about.
As the distance between potential competitors decreases, no one can relax.

At the first sign of a problem, display your weapons.
Sharks deploy as much of their bodies as possible, maximizing surface.
Lions rub themselves on each other to create a smell of the pride.
Extend, fan out, bear teeth, build dungeons. Aggression shouldn't hurt.
Once you've scared the other guy, quickly decrease appearance; save gas.
The king gets agitated, however, at this suggestion; he likes to go all the way.

Sal's dancing came out fully functioning and needed no social gestation.
Still, everyone knows the queen's fitness will be measured by Sal's survival.
The mole rat controls the sexual state of the entire community through her toiletries.
The king yawns because he isn't stimulated. The others yawn too. These are deceitful signals.
Sal observes these costly communications as the selfish herd backs into a circle.
Bleating and staring from their paranoid crescent, they scramble toward dinner.

Sal tries to conjure a signal that would scare off everyone except Mike and Stacey.
Her instincts arrive like foreign guests and are impossible to ignore. Greet or run?
Greeting the army is useless when they've got orders. Running from soldiers is stupid.
She wishes the queen might have bred with a better class of shoe-salesman.

Envy is practically impossible to notice in species which don't interact with humans.
The rarer you are, the less likely you'll be preyed upon, the less you have to lose.

Still, masquerade is the best defense; stand colored like the background, shaped like it.
Twig caterpillars who look like bird droppings avoid being picked for dinner.
Moths and fish flap erratically, appearing sick and unappetizing.
Disguise your face by painting eyes on your ass. Harlequin. Coral Snake.
Mark yourself distinctly and people will assume you are noxious. Vamp.
Fair warning comes in colors; mimic the warning and save the expensive poisons.

Fireflies go home with any beetle who sends out their wives' signals.
Each has its own flash, a particular way of turning the phrase.
Signals in drunken, dark-lit cacophonous crowds are messy and hard to discern.
The beetles easily rip their flattered hearts from their sleeves.
Turns out being "individual" is nothing more than pushing a shopping cart of cues.
The more shopping goes on, the more cues are needed to identify the deadly.

Still, antlers get costly, making Sal even more conspicuous.
Soon the imitators all have them and you find yourself needing a new cue, a.s.a.p.
A rat in trouble jumps to startle the snake. A sea cucumber turns inside out.
Some prey are so poisonous they kill themselves in the process of surviving.
No "learning" happens that way. A cricket'll tell you playing dead can backfire.
Natural selection favors anyone who can survive this pile-up of images.

Margins

Something's wrong with Sal: her calls come too late at night, too often.
She wants to do too many things over the course of a day.
She speaks endlessly into the answering machine. Then calls back.
Late at night, I stand away from the windows as she aims badly with stones.
Then the doorbell starts ringing as I lie deeply in the couch.

Would you like a ride tonight? It's awful weather, I don't mind waiting.
Maybe it's true that a person should always help others.
One's generosity is their humanity, their soul food; I guess you'd call Sal a glutton.
No one wants to grab the food out of someone's mouth or deprive them of a meal.
But Sal's a binge giver; one you suspect is off vomiting somewhere.

Anything you need or want she'll find for you; anything you don't know, she'll explain.
Even things you've barely dreamt she'll conjure.
Directions? She laughs and tells stories, going to the car to lend you her map.
Suggestions for a restaurant, a mechanic, a doctor, a quiet place to read?
Her every idea blooms more fully and perfectly than the last; her every privilege, yours.

Anyone she knows she'd love you to meet; anything she's won you can have.
Into fantasies you've never gone and desires you haven't felt, she'll coax you with ease.
A few drinks when you're lonely, a casual, methodical, flattering examination of your soul.

Fears you've never expressed she'll soothe and repackage into a common humanity.
And all with a feeling of contagious pleasure that in her you see what you might love.

Once I was stuck underground, a bad scene with God, prophecies of doom.
Sal called me to an intimate bar and led me into conversations about archetypes.
She sopped up my self-pity with careful teasing and rounds of compliments and beer.
I plunged into her consuming attention, while she deftly worked my faith.
Within an hour I saw the outline of a dungeon I'd never imagined.

Her voice is certain temptation: a path deep beneath a mountain.
See, I am a man of a different persuasion, never desiring any woman.
I thought: If I make it through this night, I don't have to see her mouth shining.
She rarely spoke about herself, only kept questions coming.
My edges started dulling and the colors around us drained of definition.

When finally she spoke of herself it was like a kid bringing favorite toys from the attic.
She made me feel careful and worthy as each piece was ceremoniously handed over.
Somehow she knew I needed these feelings and so even my helping her helped me.
Her gaze took root and her stories bore into my chest.
Still I remained suspicious, not of any real agenda, but of her childish speaking.

Yet I knew that this was the purpose: some secret reversal of healing.
And in the touching, which amounted to nothing more than listening, her words took flesh.

Here was the invitation to a fearful intimacy; that I might consider fucking her.
Her mouth, her mind, the contours of her experience—bringing all of them into warmth.
I should really stop drinking, I interrupted, calling a halt to the whole idea.

I thought if I make it out of this scene, I'll never have to see her mouth again.
It's not like she asked me for anything, I'm just a good target.
Unwillingly I took her hand, stroked her fingers, and suffered a wave of desire.
She wants me to be something I'm not, suddenly washed up in kissing her.
I must be drunk. Drunk and attracted to the perfect wrong person. God forgive.

It's getting late for me, me with my obligations and activities. She offers more help.
Endless little strings; logistical details serving no purpose but to bind me to her.
Webs of times, places, reasons to see her. The present moment can't hold what she offers.
So it stretches and disfigures, its pieces graft and splice onto upcoming days, months.
In short, I blame her for everything. For making me feel like I could stay forever.

My brain starts burning and she rushes over to put it out even as she sparks it again.
This wasn't the emergency I planned for. I'll never see her again if I make it out of here alive.
Really, I'd love to go with you, she says. I'm going to be there anyway. It's no trouble. I want to.
But days pass and I was supposed to have called her back. Every hour is an hour I don't see her.
A week becomes a week and a day. It's becoming obvious again that life is simple.

When I see her now I can tell any weight on this bridge will have to be mine.

She won't look at me. She's laughing with someone above ground at the party.
Her temptations tailor to each perfect victim. We can torture her all night.
She could come up and smile and I could look at her, touch her, take her home and fuck her.
Or ignore her and forget about her completely.

Tongues

And yet, Mike continues, she appears never to contradict anyone directly.
She's so passive she doesn't say an idea until she knows it'll work, Stacey adds.
The bar's getting crowded and they won't seat for dinner unless the whole party's there.
They leave her a message: it's too rainy to walk around, we'll do it another time.

Sal sits and waits for food. Days go by and when it passes in front of her she eats it.
She doesn't go after it. When it's there, she's suddenly hungry. She eats and has metabolism.
She speeds around for awhile. She'll sink her teeth in if your paralysis is convenient.
Then she waits again, still as stone. Barely breathing. Body temperature cold. Thoughts slow.

Others eat and drink and laugh. Others wear jewels and make history and cry. Sal watches.
Her body temperature cools as night comes on and the torches are lit along the paths.
Fire reflects in the fish-pools and the flames dance, licking the shoes of the soldiers.
They play their flutes to charm her, but of course she can't hear them, though she sways.

Underground once, her legs became of so little use as to fall off.

Bones and skulls line the damp cisterns where sound doesn't bother coming.
In this place 145 million years pass without a clue. Friends don't call again.
Sal rejected the abundance of small land mammals in order to escape her habitat.

Some of the king's guests try to catch Sal alone after dinner.
Their slithering and elongated physiques don't fool her; their hips give them away.
Unlike hers, their skulls can't protect their brains and are easily crushed.
Trying to kiss her they meet the misfortune of distensible jaws; her saliva of burning acid.

The similes grow thick as vines as Sal stands farther and farther from the action.
Her jewels lack lids and, widely, never blink; their glassiness sloughed off in slow time.
Sal only hears things traveling through the ground, ignoring the things in the air.
With her secret ear she listens to someone praying.

On shifting sand it is impossible to get a good grip, so Sal sidewinds slowly.
Her metabolism keeps her creeping; unable to sprint for long, she's careful who she knows.
The prophecy her feet feel is one man's extreme futility; his very presence someone's vanity.
Ignorant of the glitter, her tongue finds a special taste for his words rising through the ground.

Since old and new layers of skin are no longer touching, Sal secretes fluid between them.
The old waits until the new disguise is complete before coming undone. Her smile grows over.
Don't look at her when her eyes are milky, her blindness lasts a good week. She fumbles.
She's in hiding. Storing up. Saving herself. Faithful to destiny.

Later, when all are drunk, she starts splitting at the lips, her smile peeling back from the edges.
Wriggling free in the firelight, she rubs against surrounding objects: tables, candlesticks.
Now she's at her best, her sharpest hues, her brightest eyes; total iridescense.
Looking around at the colorless cast of herself, she knows what she wants.

Sal is very short-sighted. She demands without thinking through and can't judge distances.
Immobile bodies usually go unseen but his prison of prayer is exotic. She thinks she loves him.
As he called to heaven she was in the way. She shows a tongue which is long and split.
But he cannot see; he can judge her only by the sounds it makes flickering on gravel.

The ground trembles as Sal senses the infra-red of his warm body and grows meaner.
He hears, interrupting his prayer, the noise of chains, warfare, crowds above him.
Sal's tongue, disturbed, constantly beats at the dirt. She really needs his help, you see.
She insists he help her, though she could, of course, help him. There's a movie in her eyes.

She can swallow someone much larger than herself. Her stomach is a damn straight line.
He refuses to alternate any type of message with her so she answers him whole.
Sal would like to co-star in his epic, ride away on horseback. She'd like his warm mouth.
She'd like to bask in his prayer or hibernate in his face, looking his perfect likeness.

Dummies

Her first real dummy was witty, charming, looked like her. You'd swear he was alive.

Sal took care not to humiliate him, never doubling him over backward. No suitcases.
She did her unpacking offstage where no one could see the dismemberment.

From the first, Sal had completely custom controls made for him.
Seven years she spent designing his mouth. Four years on his real blinking eyelids.
She read 10 Steps to Building a Perfect Dummy but decided to hire a professional.

A taxidermist collects the best hair, eyes, tear ducts, and skin for amateur dolls.
There's a complex series of moving parts in their hollow bodies. Sal wanted deluxe.
His musculature and face should mimic hers; his expression, less ambivalent.

All day he sat for her in a child-sized chair while she danced and primped.
At first she practiced with him twenty or thirty times a day: 1. Don't move your lips.
Use the mirror to watch your mouth for any cheating: "Slay-the-ree" "Ad-then-cher."

She understood he needed to appear completely independent.
This system took time. She strove to string together words she had mastered.
She learned there is no such thing as throwing your voice, it has to be done the hard way.

As a child, Sal discovered that hearing is the most untrustworthy sense.
So she found a contrasting voice and the dummy didn't sound just like her.
And on videotape she practiced unclenching her jaw and laughing without smiling.

As the days went by, she assembled a litany of counterfeit words, a phoneme away. "Thor you I hoo-ud do anything." "I luth you there-ee nuch." His jaws flapped as she spoke. The essence of the act is that her character is real; the dummy fools everybody.

In order to keep the routine lifelike, some part of the dummy should always be moving. Sal's act has a simple plot and dummy movements follow it. Stare. Laugh. Stare. She keeps the audience engaged by alternately frightening and ignoring them.

Once Sal made the dummy do a headspin, causing demented laughter. It was the best house she played to, and even though it ruined the illusion, she profited. From then on the dummy got assembled and stuffed into his suitcase onstage as well.

She disposed of her first dummy after several years. Anything can be made to talk. Hands, socks, clouds, policemen, stars, governments, statues, train stations, dogs. Sal wanted the world to speak to her by itself.

From then on the dummy got emotionally out of control. Double takes. Crying. He went into her room and chewed at furniture. "I hate you" "I hate you like . . . " Technically, those are easy words to say. She covered her ears.

But increasingly Sal felt hunger for an audience, and stage fright turned to panic. Open with the second-best joke. Keep routines short. Be seen and not heard. But once you give it, the audience keeps the upper hand, so Sal stopped the show.

How-To's

If you pay attention, Sal can help you clean up households, schools, governments.
Anything that comes in contact with people can be returned to its original luster.

But she won't argue if you insist on doing it your own way. She won't look.
Millions of people can be wrong at once, turning untenable ideas into democracy.

On wood, some say use wax. Some say don't use wax. Surfaces grow dull with fingerprints.
Cockroaches can sense crumbs as small as two thousand times the diameter of a hydrogen atom.

Sal knows that delay does not always cause stains to become permanent performances.
Their permanence is about scrubbing. So stop it. Left alone, the stain will give up.

Adding protective shine is an incentive to free markets, a clear conscience.
But even the cleanest body is home to a billion bacteria converting secretions into body odor.

As Sal points out, you must allow soiled items to soak overnight.
For removal of ink: cover the area with earth and alcohol, wrap in plastic.

Before you blink, Sal's inspected your metal. Is it maintained?
Polish can often collect in the details, causing streaking, requiring scrubbing.

Moody houses harbor polluted air. If Sal tells you it stinks, don't drop it.
In a loose house, outdoor replaces indoor air at the rate of once per hour.

Irritants often do not leave traces; particles are hardest to detect or control.
You can use a tabletop air-cleaner, but these are less effective than open windows.

In your own best interest, use shaving cream or hairspray on urine; do not ignore Sal.
Newsprint is impossible to remove without bleach. Recycle as much as possible.

Every day: wash the dishes, put them away. Every day: pray. Dust and vacuum weekly.
Every month, focus on a special area for cleaning: mattresses, bookshelves, pictures, car.

Sal knows you're too busy to listen, or think that in your position this stuff doesn't matter.
Seasonally, take inventory of closets. Every year hold an unsparing garage sale.

Colors

Winding over orange hills, a path of pure blue. On it, Sal wears a crimson smock.
Her shiny black shoes are question marks on the stones. Sal doesn't tint her smile.
Through the window overlooking the meadows, Sal's hair turns a virgin, tarnished copper.
When you see her sitting upside-down on the yellow bench, don't look at her lack of gardening.
As vain as daylight she prepares the most violent similes in creation.
White peacocks wander the multi-colored meadows, Sal armadillo gray against them.

Purple soldiers exercise creamy stallions. Sal throws her darkest shadow there.
The husband drops the woman's bruised arm from his fingers. The saffron bruise smears off.
He calls for his soldiers. The wife pulls off her electron wig, shaking loose a laugh.
Sal in studded iodine stares for a moment until the air is a moony pepper mist.
Listening through her eyelids, Sal radiates the spectrum of invisible light.
Where she bought a kiss, the marble stairs wipe themselves clean of the mess.

COMING—OF—AGE

In principle we go — A work of art or to a hospital — A work of art or down a long corridor — Always reproducible — To see manmade artifacts — Imitated — Our mother in principle — Has always been technique

Replicas were made and there we went — Joined by third parties — In the pursuit of the hospital — Of gain — "Come leave," the agents dissimulated — The mechanical reproduction of a babe's tooth — To see — Historically — How the brain represents something new — To keep pace with printing — Our mother advanced — Intermittently — In leaps at long intervals — But with accelerated intensity toward disguise

As the Greeks first founded and stamped — We went — All others were unique — Long before any special revolutionary case — "To the hospital!" — Yet pictorial infection at the curtain of the nineteenth century — Was incurable — We traced the design — To quarantine a few rituals — Was the eye looking into a lens — Or our mother — Gone more swiftly than a hand can draw

We go but we hate to because we are breeding things ourselves and don't want to mix samples. The Scottish Longhair, the Guernsey, the seed from all the livestock she birthed from her red, peeling barn doors. The seeds are kept in a viscous substrate at room temperature; the vials held in delicate pincers. We wear special electronic gadgets that spray our unique patterns of radiation to small hand-held sensors. Our portraits are compared to our file. Only those with top-security clearance are allowed in the storage rooms. Our files are the source of verifiable truth; the closest there is to original creation. Unfortunately, the hand-written intertitles were the first to decompose, out from the center of words toward the neighboring celluloid. Likewise her gibberish mesmerizes the staff. Most of the first reels have long since rotted and only a few genetic filaments, belonging to those lucky bastards who stored their memories separately, can be injected into the herd.

For the first time we went straight to photography — Freed our homes — To the hospital — Or the process of reproduction — A sterile room —

Virtually implying the pace of speech — Flash — And our mother —*cinema muet* — Tracing the first generation of patents pending — The cone of light — "Be Grateful" — My Children — For the Gesture — Her eyes in a death flutter

The presence of the original — Patina — Her sweating forehead — An archive of the industrial century — Over here — Elicits a bow to the sphere of authenticity — Twofold and manual portrait — Cranking at an above-average speed — The birth rate — Unattainable brush-strokes choose their emulsions carefully — As we develop the contrasts of the beholder — Our mother's grainy breasts — Halfway

The hormones come powdered and we sample them with the tip of licked finger to tongue. Hmm. Can they produce the best milk? The science is astounding and forces us to abandon our instincts: to focus on melody at the price of drama. To choose the zeitgeist over the graph and deny the presence of what can't be diagnosed. Virtuosic grunts come from our instruments of artificial insemination. Hmm. We consult her only regarding the phenotypes that produce the heaviest sales. She can no longer choose her penetrations, only absorb the news, the cows squeezed upon with cold metal piping, trapped in the splintering pens. She would like to serve us her flesh, but the steroids and rubber tubing won't allow.

We go to the cathedral — Its locale in the studio or a soundstage — Or a motorized bed — To reproduce our mother — Performed in an auditorium — Or in the open air — Identical brothers echo in the drawing room — Waiting room — Where the acoustics are best — "Your presence is greatly depreciated" — Her speech is canned — A feast for every occasion — Is this really our last visit? — Her lips make air-kisses

All that is transmissible — As our mother — From the beginning manifest — The folds of sterile gauze and chiaroscuro — And what is jeopardized when the historical is affected— The ritual —The authority of religion — The old-fashioned birth canal —The aura is what withers as we — Duplicate — Over and over our Mother — Ceremonies of economy —The birth of the touched-up — Images destined to serve no one — Globally

We approach her slowly, her cranks and black casing held by rubber bands and old string, the lens dusty, bulbs and mirrors missing entirely. Only a tattered, eaten, rotted reel spills from her mouth:

> A shattering (—we go) The corridor blows in (—to) And in permitting the liquidation (—to) this is 1927 (—the hospital) I am a film walking the town disoriented (—to) My brain has moved to the mouth where the conclusions are projected (—to see) And the shut shut of my decaying aura stuffs the function of their visiting (—we go) To feel nothing is only possible while resting on a summer afternoon (—to the hospital) Every day the urge grows to get hold of an object (—to see) at close range by way of mechanical genitals (—our mother) They come to the hospital to see their mother's genitals (—we haven't) under the paper gown (—seen) Unmistakably (—her) Unarmed (—like this) Undeserved (—before)

The vials bearing seeds increase in value with the outstanding performance of the herd. We approach the bed cautiously, not wanting to scare her out of the scarecrow costume, or ignite her hair as the sun focuses through our glances. We pull back the plastic coated curtains colored orange with patterns of leaves.

Permanence is "going" — We — To such a degree — Reproduce the labor — Lose all time — As our mother did in her imaginary barn — This is manifest in the field of perception — "To see" — What in theory is only noticeable as statistics — "The hospital" is a process — Limited by characters — And statistical significance — As much for thinking as for perception — The masses adjust to the work — Technical magic — Or mothering — And produce serials from behind massive pillows — Doled to starving refugees — The cult finds newsworthy expression — The art of the smile — The scan — The rotted floorboards in the hayloft — Better sources of indoor lighting — The curve of a dead field mouse spine — The last symptoms of Rembrandt — Fixed

Her head rests heavy in our palms. Back and forth we hold her in sleep as it labors to keep from collapsing. We want to crawl up next to her but ancestral witches in other beds mock our mention of "hygiene," which of course is no more than a footnote in the last era of cool air and how her breathing is sponsored by electric cord. Her head slips to the side, her choking indicates that she may convulsively and finally remember — What — That — She named us.

We go in world history — The battery of surgeries — Parasitical dependence on generations — To the hospital — To test the educated genetic guesses— Reproduced from a photographic negative — Emancipates the farm nerve from agriculture — To see our mother —The screen will display a "?"— A last frame of heartbeat — As "certain sculptures on medieval cathedrals are invisible from the ground" — No higher exhibit is possible of belief

Bump. We hit.

Gone for the last time — En masse — To strike against her — The disputed lapse in the system — The last symptoms of an emergency — Emanates from the early stuttering of films — To see in the fleeting expression of a face — The illness of history — The resulting change in our mother — Her performance substituted by a hard plastic womb stimulated by batteries.

And where to go now — ? — Aching and bumping along the corridor — Regaining in principal — Our mother original — Wanting to say something — But reeling in — The syndicate — The fake part of cruelty — An ancient ritual of family — Nowhere more Everywhere than here — Her children won't stay for another showing — "Good riddance" — She coughs blood — And a tiny mewing — She's franchising in the next world now — The nurses get busy

SETTING, THE TABLE

On one particular [day of the week] — perhaps a Sunday by certain indexes, perhaps [a holiday] or [a day of religious observance] — but in any case a day in which all members of a group known in some languages as a family, starting together from [a set location] constrained by physical angles and bone structures, sometimes a roof here and there, gather around the ordering of a table called, for the sake of convenience, their mother's table, in her specific home, designated to strangers by [a particular number] followed by a series of [proper names] indicating street, town, country, though not necessarily referred to in casual speech as anything other than "here" or "there" — four boys (known to each other and to their mother by [specific names] but also by [4 elemental symbols or states]) endure only as long as [4 specific ideas] or [4 action verbs] before vanishing back into whatever was originally meant for them, either in the narrative or in the drama — And because people in technological ages feel compelled to reveal all things set before them, keep in mind that on the particular day in which this repast is presented, each brother sets out into the surrounding meal on a specific journey which can never be described more accurately.

[how to get someplace you've never been]

Setting out to arrive, the boys return home, losing synchronization, changing skin color, often mistaking each other for strangers. In a different way each, by returning, causes their mother, whose technologies set for them the first place. She aims her plates, glasses, flatware, sideboard, refrigerator, oven and sink — directly at the idea of each of her children. For months she ponders from the kitchen: which that, exactly how, and so creates recipes for all the mouths now before her. With her labor she brings them forth and sets them free to their places, preparing them for their complete arriving. She takes cause to urge everyone forward because things seen on mars are roving to be present, to lie pre-discovered and ready, just as bees, it is said, make mental pictures, and the tool for each is time: this unique waggle aimed at that particular audience. Similarly she cooks directions into each course. Would they stay unrevealed? The details get overlooked in the recording of the trip.

[story of the first map]

But don't they start getting excited!

On their excursions the brothers grow strong or weary, cold or brave, hungry or rich. They meet robbers, widows or children and test these topographies against repeat encounters, drawn and redrawn with imaginary rhumb lines just as mariners recorded the coasts. Out into this sea each boy launches himself — tacking and running — as if by trimming a luffing sail or coming about, each might nose his vessel into [a headlong force], [a synonym for "life"]

Surveying the expanse from their distinct advantages they are themselves surveyed. Their mother, set at table, sets all light dappling and disappears. They hurry to drop reliable anchor. Deeper into the deep which is this moment they plunge; water meets their shoes and slows them. Once on shore, sand from their past meets their eyes and blinds them. Smog, set forth by their own setting off, meets their lungs and chokes them. Grace sets past the point of [4 ways to say Grace] so that at the end of each turn they hover in a place all can see but no one can occupy. The question, "will I get there?" remains unanswerable.

first setting to the right of the head of the table

His brother   Imagine an apple orchard with trees as huge as

His brother   [the biggest hug you ever gave a man]

His brother   where the healthy hand down fruit from ropy arms (we appreciate a distinct taste)

His brother   [2 ways to know if fruit is ripe]

His brother   [3 signs that this fruit is not another]

His brother   Isn't this the perfect setting? Yet one life rejects its season: instead of a bountiful orchard as vivid as damp weather

His brother   [3 scenes from a legendary boy's life]

His brother   [3 scenes from his life]

His brother   a dotted line barely separates his sickly trunk from the meadow and so we find on this map an empty space, nameless with the exception of his roots in the way-back-when, in the once blush of his full probability.

His brother   [how "undernourished" equals "understanding"]

His brother   [5 mileposts you watch for as children grow up], [2 drawbacks of "wondering"]

His brother   In his place, where the map says nothing, we might have expected to find trees as lanky as his clothes, or eyelashes clotted like blossoms, or his drizzling hair; an orchard, a process of organization, an open reversal of decay where his probable apples should nicely grow; where little would be wasted, from

His brother   [1 way he amused you when he was little], [2 ways that bees perform "essential services"]

His brother   to jelly jars and cider and over-ripe apples for feeding horses — here, with all that should come with what should be, we nod at our plates and wait.

Ice cubes pass.

His brother   We licked his pollen sacs when he was little to stimulate him for the school bus, for windy friends, for flying friends, knowing [3 ways agriculture has benefited from technology]

His brother   knowing in the dark [how his lantern screams for bugs] and that he traced sticky juice on his palms, or in his hair, his stained teeth the color of pulp, and still he couldn't attract success. Planting and planning don't always produce fruit; especially if the breezes sleep that year, or bees are few, or he frosts up when spoken to.

His brother   [2 things to do when your child makes no friends]

His brother   [definition, "sterile"]

His brother   Why do you eat with your eyes closed?

His brother   An orchard is not this growth of a boy into a man. He thinks many things he talks himself out of, even when he cracks his petals to seek a whispering breeze. Sometimes there's no breeze and other times hurricanes, useless detail of pollen, postcards, bus fares — so that even the lantern he holds near his face, his safety blanket of unnecessary light, sputters out.

Water passes.

His brother   [definition, "fruit"]; [definition, "shadow"]

His brother   Don't peek where the fence of his imaginary self falls loose, or think

His brother   how we always knew [3 differences between him and the other boys in school] because even in the excitement of being hired for a job, any job involving [definition, "communication"] or [definition, "control"] — just good honest work like normal kids do — he always got degraded; [3 ways soil gets depleted] or [2 euphemisms for "loser"]

His brother   Why didn't he get attention for his occasional spurts — a leggy sprout, a tuft of healthy blooms? He always knew the legend by heart, and the distance chart and even [2 signs of bad earth] —

His brother   he was composed, but he never composed.

His brother   Unlike his, our petals opened flat for better landing sites. Our petals collected drinks, or offered nectar, or umbrage from the wind. Our bright blooms sent unmistakable signals to the insects; we shone and our successes grew. In our beds, flowers enjoyed promiscuity among friends. Nature has no unemployment, rather, the exploitation is total. His unemployment requires sunlight, nourishment, and a wormy plot of land.

His brotherr   In theory, the sun's energy stores in the seeds, the seeds give the energy to the apples and the apples to our own ambitions. The apple orchard appears in the legend of all sets of towns and regions, the unspoken myth of traditional, earnest values — enterprising, stable.

His brother   Even stunted and barren, the orchard attempts its name. Describe [something imponderable] or [why straight trees have crooked roots] — In other words, between water and bread, or soup and salad, try to answer his limited questions like [why the most probable messages give the least information] or [why cut twigs bend toward each other]. And even between bites, impotently listen as he describes [2 reasons maps have blank spaces] or

His brother   [7 clichés about the way life is]

His brother   Then even if he survived a few weeks on the job, his discombobulation grew; for example, his mouth fouled and his teeth fuzzed up, and the sizable feat of making a living folded into [something too small to fit in a pocket]

His brother   as he sank deep into the airless place at the bottom of [a noun]

Bread passes.

His brother   [7 kinds of silence]

His brother   Even a fertile society might have contorted under the weight of [3 behaviors of "attractive" men] and [4 reasons to call a person "weird"] so that snow falling or seven-year plagues or excessive manicure or

His brother   [2 things which scare you about the way he looks] or [1 thing he does which is not "normal"]

His brother   or even [3 synonyms for "barren"]

His brother   might have conspired to prohibit him from reproducing. None
of the other orchards contorted. He was simply never aston-
ished at a girl. He never showed [1 symptom of physical
attraction]. Alone he primped in his enclave and his compul-
sive measuring fooled everyone about his progress. (You need
only think of [3 complex machines] or [3 synonyms for
"smart"]) — And still, not even stunted fruit came off into the
baskets; his failure his only sexual action, but failure alone
cannot move him. He sways in wind but cannot travel so his
synapses have drawn into his brain stem as he rots in place.
Synonyms like [3 synonyms for "tree"] or [2 synonyms for
"kin"] are no consolation because he's already out of focus;
you'll find [2 reasons plants feel no pain] as you speak to him.

His brother   [the first sign that a seed is sprouting]

His brother   [2 reasons money doesn't grow on trees]

His brother   Yearly his thoughts dampen and are eaten out by beetles, bor-
ing. Little holes, I'm telling you, it's not his fault, only his
mental age or [4 ways to tell if someone is incompatible with
himself] or his terror, generally, of fire.

His brother   Don't stare at his lantern while he's thinking [3 types of med-
ical maps], [3 religious mottos of survival], [1 television jin-
gle] or notice

His brother   in his eyes narrowly averting, his ideas groping every ground-
crawling branch, struggling toward the blurry leaves.
Uninvited pests, drunk in lost diction, tongue-tied as the dis-
integration of the known universe, disorient him with a few
randomly cogent sentences.

Butter passes.

His brother   Some seeds arrive in his eyes. Hope they set him arriving.

His brother   But there's only one hope and he considers it loudly in his empty amphitheater. Furtively he glances at the other table settings and decides not to mention the cure. It's only a simple tearing, the slightest pull downward on a healthy branch with a twist. And then, of course, the wedge slips easily under the flap of neck skin left from his decapitation. Tape the new branch tightly to protect against weather and in a few seasons the graft is seamless. The miracle of his headless stump bears the new brain-child without even the scar of his previous mind.

second setting to the right of the foot of the table

His brother   Picture him partial as we see him, red hands impatient for [all specific names]: organic and inorganic to incinerate in his glory days, his foundry days, his white-hot lips curled open as workers probe with iron tongues, sixteen men and twelve hours long — his workday searing their palms to their hand bones, his face open-cut, we can't help but stare at his profits, enflamed — stop!

His brother   *Tccchkk* — the igniting scratch of sulfur-stick on sand, arguing to a match: Act! [4 ways to draw a bottom line] or [definition, "firefight"] as we soften close to him, this one we've looked up to, his constant but familiar threat, heat, [what it means to be caught red-handed] — backing us off like [1 way a child overachieves]

His brother   like workers, long-range, we're glad to see him returned in person from [4 military engagements] with his over-time and fancy gifts, hoping someday he won't be firing us [how sunlight damages skin] [2 ways to tell if a fire has gone out] — we instinctively reject his paychecks, brigades — we've always tried to retain something inflammable like [3 human rights]

His brother   or [4 political actions which are unmappable] while he outgrows his chair, everyone scoot back, making room

His brother   as each thing, steel off his production line, recalls the greenshaded areas on the map where wrongly we read a verdant landscape, misinterpreting [3 classical virtues] for [4 good deeds he did as a boy]

His brother   rather than [4 effects of unregulated industry] or [definition, "creep"]; in other words, we assumed [2 ways to look on the bright side] as equal to [4 white lies] while his satellites were busy putting "everything" on the table — in plain sight, like

His brother   [what it means to "fire and forget"]

His brother   his earliest school-days had forests sketched, a manic map encyclopedia — quarry stone, bicycles, dimes, skyscrapers, plumbing pipes — each symbol a folded fantasy, an occasion for pouring another I-beam. He hasn't stopped conveying him- self up-the-ladder since the first lode; it's impossible not to stare at the gargantuan leaps he makes before us, stuffing his face, flush and mobile, radiant with [2 appealing qualities of danger], occasional flashes of color; the sexy obesity of home.

His brother   Which is why he shears us and we tolerate his temper, bribed by crystals [the rights of minerals], gems formed despite the molten vulgarity he spews when asked [1 innocuous question] like could you simply say [where fire comes from]

His brother   his chin with brown rivers of corrosive hunger

His brother   as pathetic as ever we dab it up, worrying he isn't eating enough, always convinced he was underfed, constantly fooled by his "running off" of endless mouth, eroding fault-zone of his bonanza — ha! The fault just [a symptom of a mama's boy], the strain, the slump of rock, apparently stable but attached untenably to a mercurial incinerating core, a hope, [2 spurs to work]

His brother   a starving unfeedable gap, hunger reinvested, he thrusts [2 insatiable needs] into the pan and we never could dig fast enough to unmuck the dividends of [1000 industries]; keep up rocker, cupel and pulp

| His brother | [2 ways to tell if someone's full] — we're helpless as he helps himself to {14 things which fuel a fire] — wiping his smoke clean on our air, he kicks, curses and sputters — a constant irritation to our appetites — [3 ways to treat a hyperactive child] — a hill of bones licked clean wherever a corner or glance will catch them; we say "normal fault," like [3 ways heat affects soil] or [4 games he always won] |

His brother   or [why ash fertilizes]

His brother   kleptomaniac within arms-reach, take this, his sickness our contant gift

His brother   willfully forgetting [the process by which things melt]

His brother   or [why metals gain weight when they burn]

His brother   and yet of all the boys his health was most robust, and our pride in him, mother's, became measured by how far he pushed us away at honors dinners, and how we nonetheless invested in [1 thing that follows ambition like a shadow]; his future

His brother   esteemed payroll, capitalizing [the difference between a "pinch" and "strike"] and taking [10 tips for passing tests] a bit too far

His brother   [4 measures of success] [4 foolish consistencies]

His brother   we waited years for an invitation to the tour, if only to catch sight of [1 place fire is controlled], but he never called

His brother   thinking he didn't want any [definition, "family reunion"] mixing with his conglomerate; the property lines are dashed.

His brother   He demands more room, servings, continuous cutting, drilling [2 ways to burn a bridge] into our heads silently we notice [the difference between a plant and a plant] and [why rain can't squelch a fire]

Salt passes.

His brother   Running out, tiring of the food and *mommy*, our best prospec-
tor, spoiled, he continuously salts the very shaft he's rushing
— can't keep it up, he binges

His brother   forcefully assuming, politely, *gimme*

His brother   profit, after all, is merely [definition, "risk"] a hucksterism,
loosely working

His brother   as mesmerized we stare straight at him, how his gaseousness
spits, stings, mild for a moment, then grabby and fat and
lurching — a lottery — a great feat of social engineering —
he jackpots occasionally

His brother   but can't spend his, mother scurrying back and forth, we won-
der [where calories go]

His brother   without ever asking, he turns [4 types of industrial maps] into
his exact wish and reaches for it; we watch it smoke just before
he catches hold

Pepper passes.

His brother   and it burns away, we've known him as long as arm's length;
he's fat with it, high with it, he grabs up air, his girth as wide
as private property, we deed it over, letter by letter

His brother   a fire at the center is still fire, and so forth to the heart of his
thought: *there's nothing at all to me except where I'm moving;* or:
there is nothing to me except what I'm eating

His brother   his actions revealing: *my fat is all they see* or *my money* or *what
gets hungrier the more it eats . . . ?*

His brother   [the space between "action" and "bead"] the automated guid-
ance of the freest markets; "home" heat-seeking; isotherms,
"need"

Olives pass.

His brother   [why strike while the iron is hot]

His brother   *what dies without eating and eats itself to death?*

Bread passes.

His brother   Still hungrier he hisses at our plates, licking every drop from the spoons and forks, indifferent to [how a smoke alarm works] his flesh falling into the food, exploding windows

His brother   everyone's yelling: Fuck you! Sit down! *Smolder*! [why a mother loves a son no matter what he does]

His brother   he flares in exhaustion — a pass of chills — we quiet, the cold-front approaching, and for a moment imagine curling up on a soft rug near his extinction . . . Controlled, we console him, he'd be safely adored — millions of consumers napping by his memory, gazing for comfort on his two-dimensional effigy — too soon, an ice age, so cozy

His brother   he boils over, hissing as he hits the planks, climbs the curtains, pulls down the beams, the dining room descending

His brother   until we all must move, grab the tablecloth and throw it across his outraged hair, smothering it to char, winding down he panics but we won't let him up; when he's weakest we choke him off, a stagnant end, some smoke; he looks so small.

first setting to the left of the foot of the table

His brother   Forget [2 romantic notions] of evolution, the youngest one tunnels straight through: hit [6 sentimental objects] -and-run for a parking lot; his triple-A bonds, his [definition, "prodigal"] held out pridefully. He doesn't wind through town [the way a little boy runs] or carefully place a foot [the way an old woman walks] but bears down in eight unswerving lanes, unstoppable and stalled; miles of horns and overheating —

smack through the rickety wooden cradle of [2 definitions, "family"]

His brother [3 reasons noise isn't marked on maps]

His brother or property tax; when he smiles you forget [where to find the "neck of the woods"] or the way he grows so deafening. He's charming and practically convincing when explaining [2 ideals of urbanity] and [3 signs of progress] for [definition, "community"], megahertzing

His brother as traffic detours around our grace, the years pass and the work stalls: putting the table back together, picking up spilt milk, gravy, potatoes, potholes potholders droning trucks and his vision unfocusing

His brother [the way bad news travels fast]

His brother [how to hear yourself think]

His brother [5 kinds of pollution] and the rest of us, too residential, gather our wits, replacing broken dishes with older dishes

His brother so that just when we accustom to the latest scheme, build up anti-bodies, there's the next racket with [2 excuses] and [3 valuable lessons] to be learned much later

His brother [how a heart sinks]

His brother because last time we agreed [how to lend an ear] he added sound-track, laugh-track, misunderstanding [why a sound mind is a sound body]

His brother a bridge as wide as [the worst way to get caught in an act] or from here to [how a crow flies] he's waving thanks from where we'd just been in our footsteps, boot straps, front stoops, enjoying [3 places people congregate] without a single thought of making room for half-a-million of his best friends

His brother	who roll by the door everyday from [someplace] to [someplace else] commuting without reckoning [the distance between thoughts] or [3 collateral costs] or [the way a neuron builds a pathway]
His brotherr	[why we creep before we walk]
His brother	never being told about [3 accidents he was in as a child]
His brother	or stopping to think [why squeaky wheels get grease]
His brother	or [1 thing which arrives before it gets there]
His brother	or *what is built but can't be dwelt in?* — a shell where we can feel at home but from which the creature has fled.
His brother	He forgets an "open" house doesn't have the same [definition, "volume"] as an open mind or [why a snail detaches from itself]
His brother	[why empty vessels make the most noise]

A knife drops.

His brother	This time, he whispers he's losing edge on the [definition, "competition"], his hopes losing [5 words which rhyme with "skies"] the twinkle in the asphalt not quite reassuring; but what does "information" look like, anyway, he boasts [the best kind of cable] and [how to pave a way] to something
His brother	a rope-ladder, chain of being, command, [3 interpretations of dreams] he collects our hands — as wishes make us conscious, he argues [all we've ever hoped for] in our freshest Christmas
His brother	for our sakes [how the pleasure-principle becomes the reality-principle] or [2 ways to plan a financial future]
His brother	showing [how a symptom is a highway] [why life's actions can

be mapped] mistakes and all, but not [every discarded second-thought] which silent as a double agent or [2 sense perceptions] sits, disguised in the mute and irrational, our doubt of [every kind of language]

Wine spills.

His brother | so that next time the noise subsides — we are not lulled into belief, dreaming more and more about less and less

His brother | troubled sleep, asthmatic breath, cement-mixers and [4 reasons for a detour] ([a thousand opinions about things which don't matter]), gangs of petty criminals gathering by the global water-cooler — There in the speed of idling flesh, that mile-high smile and knotting hands preaching new pay-per-view reasoning, a phone-a-thon whose cause is missing, but phone in

His brother | some lull in the jackhammer, his mind an enormous tax, a traffic on-ramp

His brother | and not [1 quality of life] for us yet

His brother | we ponder [the frequency which insects use] as he mentions [something about sunsets] describing [a poem about rainbows], a way out of small towns, small minds, something more coming, a dawning, renewing, [4 athletic qualities], [2 reasons everyone needs him], [4 national fantasies] and [5 words about progress]; we'd rather discuss [2 famous strangers on the road] or [2 reasons chickens cross it] but he calls for dessert, the deserving goods of goodly people, helping themselves, therefore

His brother | [1 good reason to hate public transportation], [5 perks to traveling by car], [4 reasons to get out of town] and [3 debts that fuel an economy] — and all his special friends taking private cruises to [8 resort islands]

His brother | where everything is quiet.

His brother   Someone needs to study [why a smile is universal]

His brother   because when he smiles we forget our elbows, jamming, he
               wins us over before we remember [3 ways to stop a speeding
               train] [6 lies he told as a kid], his journey, our obsolescence
               and the junkyard of gas-stations in whose smile we hear [5
               database languages] and [definition, "speed"] — when as a boy
               he beamed, not one of us could resist hopping in for the ride.

His brother   So he learned to avoid [5 ways a noise can be seen] — quick

His brother   an instant replay.

The oven-timer rings.

His brother   [1 reason something gets numb]

His brother   [2 causes of hearing loss]

His brother   replay the scene: stray dogs or bullies recede

His brother   grinning, or "listen" or [another vision]: [something every
               heart desires] he'd like us to be first on the block, it could be
               ours, he'll sell it back, the neighborhood is changing, he's seen
               [the face of the future] and it looks like

His brother   accelerating, while we think, no — [3 things found on a traf-
               fic "island"] — trespassing, or

His brother   [what a map predicts]

His brother   his deafening face, we shake our heads, stalling him — as
               sudden as our silence, he shifts into lobbying, his statistics
               logically arguing [3 unfair standards of behavior], our collec-
               tive inaction; now he's detouring a child's tantrum, breaking
               into tears, a baby howling: he was only trying to *help*, he
               doesn't understand why we're yelling, though we're not, or
               [why people even use language] or [2 kinds of sabotage]; he

thought we'd be proud to have [the sound of opportunity
knocking]

His brother   perhaps we don't understand [a hell] would be [a place] with-
out [2 accidents], [10 exits], [3 excruciating noises] or [4 sud-
den commotions] — where every model sells out, trading up
values: [1 quiet place] which others might call boring but
which is [1 kind of setting]. He hates tables — any slowing
— dinner as he imagines it, commuting through some eye-
sore washboard backroads, out the backdoor, all the old will be
new again, he almost sings, random access finishlines, for
miles the refrain, selling doors to doors.

second setting to the left of the head of the table

His brother   The other has nothing to say and says nothing. Calmly he
passes things which pass him, carrying what needs carrying.
When he spills a glass, drops a fork, his carelessness finds no
apology, maybe an inviting laugh as if nothing happened.
Radiant in politeness he keeps his hands on his linen napkin,
touching his mouth delicately, we can't help watching each
wave his fingers make. He gives no mind to [4 things people
wish for] but pulls only what pulls him, filling harbors with
his carefree indecisions, nodding and tossing his head around,
he leans in and then checks out. He's a thousand times as great
as us but without any noticeable successes. Only in beauty do
people acknowledge him; gazing in awe upon his sloppiness,
to hear where he's been, what he's done or seen — all to watch
his skin, his perfect features, move. But he dredges up no
ambition, even going so far as hiding the few wrecks he's col-
lected in [9 undiscovered places]

His brother   [6 ways to tell if water is near]

His brother   Everyone vies to sit next to him; all the little nieces blushing,
slicking their long hair down, clinging to his baggy jacket

His brother   he occupies the wildest seat, mellowing in the deepest basins,
we know him as the handsome one, cool and aloof, the party-

boy. And though there are [2 ways to tell if a word has a posi-
tive connotation] he generally goes along with
[definition,"interpretation"] because he knows [the difference
between *exquisite* and *useless*] and that we don't possess the
technology to fathom anything deeply.

His brother   He lifts a hand to help but he doesn't care for what. He pays
no attention to the guests, rocking their boats, filling their
cups and when he naps, his tussled hair makes the children
giggle and he doesn't fix it. He can be everything women
want, and delicately hold the babies. When he drinks and gets
sloppy, he lumbers off to bed. Over time he shows off his
[1000 colors] over [5 geologic ages] and we admire him in
every changing light, imagining that someday [1 special per-
son] will catch his attention, while pretending not to want it.

His brother   Ask him [1 question] and you'll get [1 zillion answers] — but
he'll capsize any idea you think is sound and you'd better
know [how to steer in rough weather] before approaching him
with [4 things which float], [2 abstract nouns] or

His brother   there are [4 ways even the best swimmer can drown] and [3
nautical sayings] reflecting [6 kinds of indifference] and all his
ever-changing constancy.

His brother   He embraces us even as we hold him off, holding our breath,
building breakers. It's true [how many hours he spent alone as
a kid] and how he was always welcomed with closed fists. Like
[a dead language] we don't know his face, sometimes clear,
often clouded with stormed-up sand or dirt, once or twice red
with blood, even on perfect days or [the most pristine beaches]
— unreadable, and therefore unsafe.

His brother   We think he's never forgiven us for not learning to swim —
but he doesn't care

His brother   preferring we'd just stay out of his business, which is no-busi-
ness altogether.

Candles go out.

His brother   he shows [4 types of waves] and violent storms, but

His brother   he thinks we can't understand [definition, "pattern integrity"] or [what moves without getting anywhere] —

His brother   what he ever says, or even [3 ways to tell if someone's speaking]

His brother   — all accompanied by the organized sounds of wind — or are those [2 sea birds] migrating?

His brother   When he was young we called experts in to map [all the tributaries of a sea] — analyzed, refrigerated, sampled, and compared: [2 bodies of water] to [3 ways to tell if you're having a feeling] — but he never spoke up when asked what he preferred, or how was school, or what he wanted for his birthday; [all the experiments in the world] produced no significant science out of him

His brother   he answered seventeen questions if he answered one

His brother   though millions pay some heed to him, watch, adore, travel with him — he's welcome in every town, a home to stay in as long as he wants, people think they've really gotten to know him, thinking all about him when he's gone

His brother   contemplating [3 ways philosophy deals with "beauty"] and [why things appear larger underwater] and the more he knows and doesn't know [the word for "wave" in french] the more they love him, noting every coming and going, in as many books as there are days. What pleasure he gives without a thought

Dinner grows cold.

His brother   we'd like to ask what he's been thinking

His brother [2 common questions] for an answer wait, he only beats softly against the table

His brother whole, as always, and entirely in pieces; hot coming, cool circling words brought up submerge under his brow etched with evening shadows — aged with wrinkles and then smooth in the morning — he folds back into himself, pounding the floor in a steady rhythm eroding

His brother how we are small considering [2 ways to tell if a glass is half full] and yet constituted of his same chemistry, almost lost with unstated love

His brother his mind permanently changing, enticing, blank, [4 reasons a child is called dumb] or stupid or unthinking, in need of managing, yet we've learned his unique way of speaking without speaking, appreciate at least [1000 metaphors] in every gesture

His brother some gorgeous rage or chiseled melancholy, he wants [1 thing] one minute and [1 thing] another while he means to say nothing or [everything] at once and we don't love him, our hankies sopped with heaving breath as we skulk the widow's walk — for when he finally rolls in we don't know how to talk to him, washed up on shore like he's so sure who we are, without any comprehension what that means himself.

His brother Calm but he could wipe us out, or [4 island countries]

His brother to pass the time —

His brother that's enough now: decide. Decide [1 thing to say] dear, just decide [1 thing]. Do you think we'd reject you if you made some sense — we understand [2 reasons water cannot be divided by a stroke]

His brother or [how to say two things at once] and

His brother [how a cactus drinks in a draught], even

His brother   [2 ways a map is not a mirror] and [a mirror is not the sea]

His brother   But when a man is drowning, mustn't he at some point think: *what is thinkable is potential, what is potential must be unlocked, what is unlocked is revealed, what is revealed is transformed, what is transformed is available, what is available is named, what is named is mapped, what is mapped is findable, what is findable is fixed, what is fixed is illusory, what is illusory is magical, what is magical is slightly ugly, what is ugly is stubborn, what is stubborn is beautiful, what is beautiful is disappearing, what is disappearing is dying, what is dying is disordered, what is disordered is unknowable, what is unknowable is secret, what is secret is unrevealed, what is unrevealed is what's possible, what's possible is what most people think about* when he's with them.

His brother   [4 ways beauty is a lie]

His brother   [how water can be set on fire]

His brother   he claims no name for his lack of position, that we'd circle him until he's forced to choose [a location] — perhaps he makes the journey we all do; vacillations cause him to look still, like he's mocking us for all our trouble finding [definition, "home"], too easy an ancestry

His brother   [2 ways to know if you're moving]

His brother   we can't keep him from leaving or find him out, no matter how many times he shows up, showing [why where you stand depends on where you sit]

His brother   or [4 ways love can kill]

His brother   [5 good reasons to tell lies as a child]

His brother   and [2 times light tricks your eyes]

His brother   saying nothing about [why water is artless]; he has no defense, no appetite. He has no hands to clasp, or tears. He has not one

138

mind in his body; his body was never hungry. The bells ring and are beautifully rung. But he has a trillion faces without the benefit of portraits. He can't decide when his life depends on it. He doesn't know when to say

His brother [a famous "paradox"]; good-bye.

His brother He's gone already but he can't decide to tell us. We're so used to seeing him without anything to see in him; [3 things that happen as people age], [definition, "solid"]; we think he's unfounded, and yet inside our veins [the percentages of blood]

Water whistles.

His brother With his gaze that reveals nothing he escapes — first our mother, then conceding journeys can't be made, we can't form a bridge across [1 small thing] or [1 clear idea]: [3 names for america]. So in the meantime consider [10 kinds of change] which make all change visible, or [1 definition, "anything"]; [the difference between returning and arriving]

IMPOTENCE OF FIRST LINES

fair lovely "boy," of super-spicy dreams   844
Fashionable prosperity of poverty   187
Feelings feelings feelings   298
For love he offered his silent perfect wor(l)d   764
For love, I grow all dumb and hopeless   382
Forbear, bold youth, all's Heaven here,   398
Foreclose the ranch? her boots have walked out there   298

Gay little Girl-of-the-Diving-Tank   291
Gay, the warrior's domestic calm, not   265
God in me is the fury of bare health   166
God, on us thy mercy's slow   366
Grain-mother, thou art still our cunning: language   182
Great-winged, perceive in coffee tremors   336
Guys with all the innocence of immanent disasters   588

Hail, Happiness, a flourescent all-night store,   776
Hank, we miss you here in Brooklyn   187
He bathes his penis in a warm excuse   387
He dreamed that he bestrode the sun   198
He fumbles at your Soul   189
Heard us that shriek?   874
Hence, Cupid! with your virtual toys,   987
Her name is Sally   241
Her name is Ursula   653
His is a loose possessive   983
His sad brown bulk sulks dark as trash   749

I is one in Rome   337
I am not that human,   879
I am that serpent-hunting cat   923
I am the pothole   456
I am too nasty, too raw a thing for you,   256
I danced for Herod, yes. My mother's eyes   145
I did not live until this time   67
I did not think you'd stop to smell that smell   101
I get disability but don't pay rent   234
I had a sudden orgasm in the night,   124

Me, me, me   505

Men go to women mutely for their peace;   701

Mild and huge and wrong,   907

Mine eyes have seen the glory of the coming of the Lord;   307

My mom left home without her purse   504

My grandmothers ate strong men for lunch   813

My Queen her sceptre did lay down,   305

Narrower than vows, into thy bedroom fly   122

Never the slant of a dog's last whine   900

New is the franchise of Heaven   515

Next stop, the counties of "Sal will Remember" —   801

Next Hank calls up looking for a clue: 713

No discernable sign   301

No Rack can torture m e—   207

Nor the waitress of Ogalalla   508

Now as I grow slow and fond of food,   401

Now let no charitable hope   551

O she who guesses the motel number right   503

O you who are my heavenly pain of Hell,   204

Observe how my stomach growls, it is   303

Often rebuked, yet always back returning   404

Oh, she will be sorry for that word!   804

One day, not soon, you will find a note   718

One day, Amorous Bystander,   902

One face stares back from all the postcards,   283

One wept whose favorite CD was scratched   338

Only a virgin can tell a life story,   992

Play a three-way melody, untie night's hands   411

Praise makes nothing but old habits   773

Pride takes no prisoners, you'll come freely   666

Remember, Ursula, you broke my couch   298

Remember Hank, even Chief Justices take shits   328

Remember Sally considering the Virgin Mary   233

Z atomic number   307

z: third of x, y and z; third variable in a tertiary equation   209

Zeitgeist, do you make deals with the market?   801

Zero never makes a number grow   505

Zero down, no monthly   718

zoos and none for me   87

Zymosis, O wanderer, lead us out of order   1